GLADESMEN

The Florida History and Culture Series

Gladesmen

Glen Simmons and Laura Ogden

UNIVERSITY PRESS OF FLORIDA

GATOR HUNTERS,

MOONSHINERS,

AND SKIFFERS

Gainesville Tallahassee Tampa Boca Raton Pensacola Orlando Miami Jacksonville

Copyright 1998 by the Board of Regents of the State of Florida
Printed in the United States of America on acid-free paper
All rights reserved

03 02 01 00 99 98 6 5 4 3 2

LIBRARY OF CONGRESS CATALOGING-IN-PUBLICATION DATA
Simmons, Glen.
Gladesmen / Glen Simmons and Laura Ogden.
p. cm. —(Florida history and culture series)
Includes bibliographical references and index.
ISBN 0-8130-1573-1 (cloth)
1. Everglades (Fla.)—Biography. 2. Everglades (Fla.)—Social life and customs.
3. Everglades (Fla.)—Description and travel. I. Ogden, Laura. II. Title. III. Series.
F317.E9S56   1998
975.9'39—dc21   97-51425

The University Press of Florida is the scholarly publishing agency for the State University
System of Florida, comprised of Florida A & M University, Florida Atlantic University,
Florida International University, Florida State University, University of Central Florida,
University of Florida, University of North Florida, University of South Florida, and
University of West Florida.

University Press of Florida
15 Northwest 15th Street
Gainesville, FL 32611
http://nersp.nerdc.ufl.edu/~upf

The Florida History and Culture Series includes important works devoted to understanding the state's rich history and diversity. Accessible and attractively designed, each book will focus on various topics of historical interest, such as the environment, politics, literature, material culture, and cultural studies.

Edited by Gary R. Mormino and Raymond Arsenault

Al Burt, *Al Burt's Florida* (1997).

Marvin Dunn, *Black Miami in the Twentieth Century* (1997).

Glen Simmons and Laura Ogden, *Gladesmen: Gator Hunters, Moonshiners, and Skiffers* (1998).

CONTENTS

Gladesmen: Gator Hunters, Moonshiners, and Skiffers is the third volume of a new series devoted to the study of Florida history and culture. During the past half century, the burgeoning population and increased national and international visibility of Florida have sparked a great deal of popular interest in the state's past, present, and future. As the favorite destination of countless tourists and as the new home for millions of retirees and other migrants, modern Florida has become a demographic, political, and cultural bellwether. But, unfortunately, the quantity and quality of the literature on Florida's distinctive heritage and character has not kept pace with the Sunshine State's enhanced status. In an effort to remedy this situation—to provide an accessible and attractive format for the publication of Florida-related books—the University Press of Florida has established the Florida History and Culture series. As coeditors of the series, we are committed to the creation of an eclectic but carefully-crafted set of books that will provide the field of Florida studies with a new focus and that will encourage Florida researchers and writers to consider the broader implications and context of their work. The series will include standard academic monographs, works of synthesis, memoirs, and anthologies. And, while the series will feature books of historical interest, we encourage authors researching Florida's environment, politics, literature, and popular and material culture to submit their manuscripts for inclusion in the series. We want each book to retain a distinct "personality" and voice, but at the same time we hope to foster a sense of community and collaboration among Florida scholars.

The natural wonder known as the Everglades has been a subject of enduring fascination, for naturalists and ecologists, for frontier buffs, and for countless others who have felt the strange allure of hidden and remote places. Over the centuries this unique ecosystem adapted to innumerable natural and man-made disasters, penetrations and explorations, the construction of roads and canals, the follies of agribusiness, and the siphoning of water and other precious natural resources. Through it all, the region supported a small but distinct strain of human habitation. This diffuse band of inhabitants traditionally included a diverse assortment of Seminoles, African Americans, West Indians, and settlers of European extraction. Relying on a combination of trapping, fishing, pluming, alligator hunting, and, in more than a few cases, smuggling, these settlers managed to eke out a living from the lowlands and shallows of southern Florida.

Since the creation of the Everglades National Park in 1947, national policy and environmental regulations have restricted patterns of life and work in the Glades. But there was a time, stretching from the mid-19th century to the mid-1940s, when the gladesmen roamed the marshes and sloughs and hammocks of the region unfettered by law or "civilized" restraint. Free to experience, to enjoy, or to exploit the full range of the Glades habitat, they lived well beyond the margins of mainstream America. The unique culture fashioned by these men and women helped to inspire the elegant prose of Marjorie Stoneman Douglas, the author of the classic folk history *The Everglades: River of Grass* (1947); and four decades later it animated Loren G. "Totch"

Brown's captivating memoir *Totch* (1993). The books by Douglas and Brown allowed thousands of readers to taste the literary and cultural waters of the Glades, but many were left thirsting for more.

Fortunately, thanks to the collaborative efforts of Glen Simmons and Laura Ogden, unsated readers now have access to an additional spring of memory and lore. Born in the Everglades in 1916, Simmons has spent his entire life in the "river of grass." A master skiff builder and alligator hunter, and one of the Glades' most sought-after guides, he came to maturity during the 1930s and 1940s, the last years of the pre-Park era. A direct link to a culture that has largely disappeared, he is a born storyteller and an able chronicler. Somehow, despite the ravages of wind and water and the press of daily life, he was able to produce and preserve a series of journals and notebooks that document his experiences in the Glades. And, to the benefit of us all, he allowed Ogden, a family friend and anthropologist, to rework his notebooks into a coherent, flowing narrative and to conduct a series of interviews that flesh out the story of his early life. The result is a remarkable work of autobiography and cultural reclamation. The lost world of the early and mid-twentieth century Glades comes alive in Simmons's reminiscences and reflections. Through his words we can recover a significant piece of Florida's past while absorbing an object lesson in environmental philosophy. With Ogden's help and guidance, Simmons has crafted a cautionary tale about a beautiful but fragile expanse of land and sky and water. *Gladesmen* takes us to an unforgettable but endangered region, a place where nature and humanity coexisted in precarious and unsteady balance, a place not unlike our own.

Raymond Arsenault
Gary R. Mormino
Series Editors

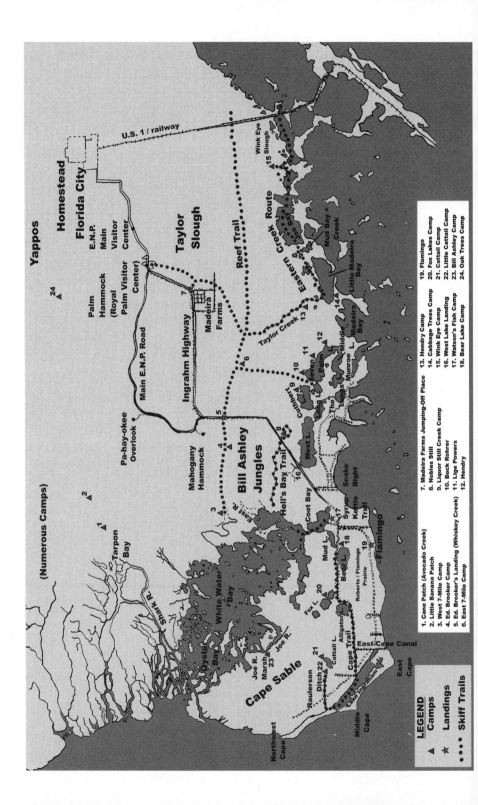

We are reaching the end of an era in Everglades history. Not an end in the geological or environmental sense but the conclusion of a more elusive historical record, one sustained within the living memory of only a few individuals. Glen Simmons's recollections of early Everglades life is one such record. Born in 1916, Glen began hunting and camping in the southern Everglades in the 1920s. His stories, which are presented in his own words, represent the central narrative of this book. Glen envisioned this book to be a tribute of sorts to the men who taught him the skills necessary for backcountry survival in the Everglades. And so his stories are filled with tales of alligator hunters, moonshiners, and the camps that these men kept along various water routes within the Everglades interior. While his account is often humorous, Glen's stories are at the same time veiled with a nostalgia for a lifestyle that was, more often than not, buggy, tough, and solitary — and now practically untenable. What emerges from this personal history is a rare portrait of both the environment and the culture of the southern Everglades prior to the establishment of Everglades National Park in 1947.

From afar the Everglades' endless prairies of gray-green sawgrass, punctuated by the occasional tree-covered island, seem deceptively concrete. But after your first step into the glades it quickly becomes clear—as your feet are enveloped by soft muck and water—that these grassy vistas are not what they initially appear. This moment of discovery underscores the system's most fundamental element: water. At one time, seasonal rains would force the waters of Lake Okeechobee to spill over its southern shore; these waters then would flow slowly southward flooding expansive marshes and sloughs and finally seep unfettered into the mangrove forests bordering the Gulf of Mexico and Florida Bay. Even today during the dry season, the system's interior glades and resident wildlife are nourished by water running through deeper drainage channels, or sloughs, and pooling in shallow ponds. These inland glades give way to a band of coastal mangrove swamps twenty miles wide in places, where fresh and salt water mingle.

Attempts at "reclaiming" the Everglades for agriculture began as early as 1881, when a Philadelphia millionaire Hamilton Disston succeeded in draining more than fifty thousand acres of marsh south of Lake Okeechobee. Florida governor Napoleon Bonaparte Broward expanded Disston's earlier reclamation efforts by establishing the Everglades Drainage District in 1907. The key to Broward's plan was the creation of four major canals (West Palm Beach Canal, Hillsborough Canal, North New River Canal, and the Miami Canal), which were dredged through the Everglades, connecting Lake Okeechobee to the Atlantic Ocean (Light and Dineen 1994, 55). Although these canals facilitated agricultural growth in the northern Everglades, flooding (which was particularly devastating after the 1926, 1928, and 1947 hurricanes) continued to restrict development. In response to the continued flooding, the emphasis of the state's water management practices shifted from Everglades reclamation to flood control (Light and Dineen 1994).

Although flood control measures have been in place since the late 1920s, for the past forty years the Central and Southern Florida Project, a consolidated state and federal water management plan (involving numerous levees, water storage facilities, and drainage canals), has played a critical role in the transformation of this water-based landscape (Light and Dineen 1994). The environmental and social consequences of these latter-day efforts span less than a single lifetime. Glen Simmons's words best convey the absolute impact this development had on the greater Everglades system as he asks:

Does anyone ever think or wonder what this country was like before development? When you're speeding along on the expressways and there's little to see but buildings that are getting thicker and bigger all the time, do you wonder what was here just a few years ago? Although it's commonly known, it was a wilderness just a hundred years ago, and a man could lose himself mentally for days without meeting anyone. Birds would fly up ahead of him, deer would jump, wary otters busy digging crawdads, quails whistling, turtles in and around the gator holes, even turkeys, a panther now and then, and fish in every hole. Now much is gone. Even in my time, since 1916, a lot of the country was still producing most things of the flora and fauna. I wonder sometimes, am I the only one that's saddened by man's takeover and ruination of this large wilderness, now gone forever! Surely not, but so few even realize it.

In writing this book, we attempt to offer a glimpse into the culture of the people who perhaps knew this complex system best—the gladesmen (as they mostly were men) who spent their lifetimes negotiating the Everglades' watery terrain prior to the establishment of Everglades National Park.[1]

The term "gladesman" was not consistently used by locals as a description for people living in the Everglades backcountry. Rather such labels as "swamp rats," "glades hunters," and the more ubiquitous "crackers" appear more often in both popular speech and text. My use of the term "gladesman" stems from a letter written by John S. Lamb Sr. to the manager of the Loxahatchee National Wildlife Refuge in the mid–1970s. Lamb employed the term self-referentially to describe the lifestyle of the people who hunted and camped in the northern Everglades, saying, "Three professional gladesmen were working the Refuge Area when we began frog hunting there. Edgar Sorenson, a truly amazing woodsman who had escaped from a correctional school in Pennsylvania, entered the Glades at the age of fifteen and spent the rest of his life there. He really was the Paul Bunyan of the Glades. He harvested whatever commodity [was] produced by the Glades which returned the best price at the time, whether it be otter pelts, gator skins, frog legs, or moonshine whiskey!" As Lamb's description suggests, living in the Everglades was similar to frontier life once common to wilderness areas throughout the United States—where simple ingenuity, hard work, and the bounty of the wild provided the stuff of daily life.

More specific, the lifestyle of South Florida's gladesmen resembles the culture of the people who lived in other wetland areas in the southeastern United States, such as the Okefenokee Swamp in southeastern Georgia. Francis Harper, a well-known naturalist, lived and worked among the "swampers" of the Okefenokee from 1912 to 1951. In his *Okefinokee Album,* posthumously edited by Delma E. Presley, Harper lovingly documents the folk expressions, ballads, and daily struggles of the Okefenokee people who farmed and hunted the swamp's pine-and-hammock-covered islands, until the swamp became a wildlife refuge in 1937.[2] Harper first encountered the Okefenokee swampers in the spring of 1912. He arrived at Billys Island past midnight, after being poled for twelve hours through the swamp's dense cypress, and his first impressions of these swampers echo Glen's description of glades life in South Florida. Harper reports:

> Morning presented an extraordinary pleasure. We observed unobtrusively the manner of life of the only human inhabitants of the remote interior of the Okefinokee [*sic*]. I felt that the lives of these sober, self-reliant people reflected the true freedom of the wilderness, no less than its solitude and privations. . . . They and the ever increasing members of the second and third generations

had continued to draw a livelihood from the manifold resources of the swamp. The longleaf pines furnished the timbers of their dwelling; the sandy loam of the clearing produced an annual supply of corn, sweet potatoes, and several smaller crops such as "pinders" (peanuts) and sugar cane; in the surrounding woods their cattle and razor-backed hogs found sustenance.

But no small part of their daily fare was derived from the wildlife around them. Deer, raccoons, opossums, rabbits, and squirrels . . . fish, soft-shelled "cooters" (turtles), wild turkeys, bobwhites, and many of the larger water birds—all were secured for the table whenever opportunity offered. (1981, 38)

Similarly, South Florida's marshes, sloughs and mangrove country provided gladesmen with a steady supply of game and fish for subsistence, as well as a link to the greater cash economy. The region's abundance of deer, rabbits, turtles, salt and freshwater fish, wood storks, coots, and wild ducks afforded gladesmen a consistent diet "in the meat line," as Glen says, while on hunting trips in the backcountry. This game also formed a staple for gladesmen's families, who lived in small communities along the periphery of the Everglades or at the frontier outpost of Flamingo. The hide and pelt market often represented a gladesman's sole means of obtaining an income, as described by Glen in chapter 3. Market demands determined the gladesman's participation in this cash economy, where fashion often dictated the demand for and price of plume feathers, alligator hides, and otter and raccoon pelts. As Glen makes clear, the fluctuations in the market demand for hides and pelts structured the extent to which gladesmen hunted and the type of game they sought.

The landscape of the Everglades must be understood as more than a mere backdrop to the culture of the gladesman. On the one hand, they were keen observers of this wilderness—spending weeks at a time walking across endless sawgrass marshes, setting camp on slightly higher hammock-covered islands, and poling flat-bottomed skiffs through labyrinths of mangrove forests. As their livelihoods depended upon the rich bounty of the Everglades wildlife, gladesmen necessarily monitored the seasonal fluctuations in the region's game. They were also

Glen, holding ducks and an otter, in a Seminole War–era dugout canoe at Madeira Farms in the Taylor Slough, 1932.

able to interpret subtle signs in this landscape (such as slight depressions in the mud, the presence of certain birds, or specific odors) to track their prey.

Their reading of these signs and their complete immersion within this environment often granted gladesmen a unique insight into the workings of this complex ecosystem. The landscape was central to their daily experience, as their self-imposed isolation in the Everglades backcountry provided them with scant other diversions. At the end of the day, gladesmen often gathered around campfires and smoking smudge pots, some sipping moonshine, to rehash their observations, to speculate, and to tell tall tales. Although most of these men received little formal education, they well understood the complexities and variations of this environment. John S. Lamb offers *one* explanation for the evolutionary formation of Everglades bayheads:

> From information from my father and other Gladesmen who knew the Glades long before my time and my own experience, I am thoroughly convinced the Glades were really once a "sea of grass." In fact, most of the original islands were started by the great herds of alligators, which migrated, from the many cypress swamps along the edges of the marsh area. The gators would build a small island of mud, muck, and sawgrass to an elevation above the water level for nesting sites. This bit of construction saved the female gators the trip to the shallow edges for nesting season. Soon after the nesting islands are built the terrific growth of vegetation begins, including willow, myrtle, bay, and rubber trees in about that order. (Lamb, mid–1970s)

Yet describing the gladesmen's relationship to the environment in terms of "observation" suggests that they lived somehow outside of this system, which isn't quite accurate. For as the term "gladesman" implies, the men whose survival depended upon the Everglades were linked to the environment in a more essential sense. When anthropologists speak of "culture," they often mean the more concrete building-blocks of daily life: the material components of a community, ritual practices, family structure, etc. Yet understanding the relationship between a group's identity and its landscape—a much more abstract concept—is of equal significance. Therefore, it is important to realize that a gladesman's identity, or sense of self, is fundamentally connected to the Everglades wilderness. In this book, we show not only how the gladesmen's cultural practices, such as hunting techniques, relate to a greater historical tradition, but also how the stories they told about this landscape correspond to their own understandings of self and community.

In the gladesmen's Everglades, what seems to be an innocuous variation in the landscape may actually reveal a hidden concordance of personal and community history. In fact, the stories gladesmen told about themselves became almost superimposed upon the physical features of the region's glades, marshes, and hammocks. Gladesmen understood the Everglades backcountry through these narratives, which are now all but lost. The names that they used for the system's sloughs, prairies, and their own camps were often derived from these stories. As a result, these place-names hint at the depth of the gladesmen's historical and personal relationship to the environment. As gladesmen navigated this complicated terrain without the aid of maps, they created these place-names, like narrative shorthand, to structure their travels. While moving through the actual physical landscape of the Everglades, gladesmen were also traveling through and continuously reevoking the history of their community.

Numerous naturalists, scientists, photographers, surveyors, and gentlemen adventurers relied upon gladesmen to lead them through the region's mangrove swamps and interior glades. Vast expanses of Everglades topography remained unmapped or little known until the 1950s, leaving the region's famed bird rookeries, mangrove swamps, and backcountry lakes and rivers virtually off-limits to nonnatives. Without a doubt, the technical reports and more popular accounts stemming from these explorations, dating back to the late 1800s, would not have been possible without the assistance of local guides. Glen Simmons's prolonged service as a guide for Dr. Frank Craighead Sr. was perhaps the final example of this relationship (Craighead 1968,

1972). Yet when the service of a guide was mentioned in such publications (which was rare), their essential contributions to the process of scientific discovery, or simply even wildlife reportage, was considerably downplayed. In fact, descriptions of gladesmen's culture sometimes served as a sort of comic relief or example of local color to the authors' more authoritative investigations. The work of Charles Torrey Simpson (1920) and Herbert K. Job (1905) represent notable exceptions to this generalization, with both writers expressing gratitude for their guides' rugged self-sacrifice. After Job's guide, who had become quite ill during their journey, led him back out of the Cuthbert Rookery, Job admits, "Without the guide I am sure I could never have found my way out of that swamp, even after being conducted in . . . poor, faithful fellow" (1902, 81–82).

Glen's experiences typify the traditional life of the South Florida gladesman. After his father died, he began accompanying much older men into the Everglades backcountry at an early age. From this diverse group, Glen learned to track game, skin alligators, build glade skiffs, and, more likely than not, tell a good story. While alligator hunting provided Glen with his most consistent form of income, he often was "just trying to live," as he says, while camping for weeks at a time in the Everglades. A severe economic collapse occurred in South Florida in the mid–1920s, and it continued unabated through the 1930s. For those such as Glen who lived along the perimeter of the Everglades during this period, the richness of the glades often provided their only source of income and subsistence.

Although Glen continued to hunt alligators and camp throughout South Florida's glades country until the 1960s, the establishment of Everglades National Park in 1947 obviously altered traditional glades culture considerably. Gladesmen could no longer keep permanent camps within the park's boundaries or set fires on the Everglades prairies—a practice traditionally carried out during the wet season to increase game density within an area. While poaching within the park became a flagrant problem for a number of years after the park's establishment, many locals moved elsewhere to hunt in nonprotected areas. Other factors during this period also contributed to the end of traditional glades culture: The relative prosperity of the postwar years facilitated commercial development in the area, thus providing less tenuous sources of income. Additionally, increased drainage efforts and better leveling equipment suddenly made farming on land along the park's boundaries tenable. At the same time, it became harder for traditional gladesmen, "glade-skiffers" as Glen calls them, to compete with the hordes of weekend hunters who used airboats, small airplanes, and glades buggies to run down their prey. For these reasons, we specifically narrowed the scope of this book to the period prior to the park's establishment (roughly from the late 1920s through the 1940s).

Throughout the years, Glen jotted down his observations of glades life in a series of pocket-sized notebooks. These small notebooks are filled with things he saw in the Everglades, humorous anecdotes about people he hunted and camped with, and songs that he has written. He used these notes to help him fill a number of larger spiral-bound notebooks with a sort of stream-of-consciousness Everglades history. For someone who has spent the majority of his lifetime outdoors and not at a desk, Glen's efforts represent a monumental task. Together, Glen and I organized his writings into four chapters, based on loosely defined topics. After this outline was established, we supplemented his writings with transcripts from a series of interviews I conducted with him during the summer and fall of 1995. Integrating these interviews into Glen's written text was not difficult, as he writes in the same "voice" in which he speaks. In editing the text, we have tried to retain the spirit of the project—which is about remembering. Repetitions in phrasing and the narrative's often elliptical quality reflect the role memory played in the text's construction, as well as the oral quality of Glen's writing.

I have written a brief introduction to each of Glen's chapters in an attempt to place each chapter's theme within an historical and cultural context. The endnotes offer explanations for certain archaic or vernacular expressions and provide further information on a number of historical events. In some cases, I have cross-referenced Glen's narrative with archival information to verify some of his observations. This secondary source material also appears in the endnotes. This project was a uniquely collaborative effort, and Glen has read, commented upon, and helped guide the research for these other sections—although any inaccuracies remain my own.

*   *   *

My own sense of respect and wonderment for Florida's Everglades was given to me by Glen and his wife, Maxie, whom I have known throughout my life. As a child they allowed my brother and me to tag along with them on long walks in the glades and fishing trips on Florida Bay, all the while carefully pointing out the subtleties of this unique wilderness. This privileged relationship has informed and been fundamental to all aspects of the book's construction.

This project would not have been possible without the gracious help of a number of people. First, we would like to thank William B. Robertson Jr. of Everglades National Park for his detailed comments and insightful suggestions during various stages of the project. John Craighead also carefully read the manuscript, offering both helpful suggestions and kind encouragement. Thomas Lodge reviewed the manuscript for the Press and his comments were very insightful. Walter Meshaka of Everglades National Park provided research and archival support. Glen Nesbit furnished original art for the glade skiff plans located in the appendix. Alexander Sprunt IV graciously allowed us to publish a number of photographs that belonged to his father, Alexander Sprunt Jr., who was an assistant director of the National Audubon Sanctuary prior to the establishment of Everglades National Park. Patrick Walker generously helped with the design and subsequent revisions of the map on page xii. Arva Moore Parks provided additional photographs for the book. Jennifer Furman, of Pitman Photo Supply, and William Losner helped with the reproduction of the archival photographs. Peter Frederick and David Swetland offered helpful technical advice on the glade skiff plans. I also would like to thank my family for their endless encouragement and enthusiasm, particularly my father, John C. Ogden, for his editorial advice and many words of wisdom.

Laura Ogden

The Long Glade

C H A P T E R   1

Born in 1916, Glen Simmons grew up on Long Glade, a small settlement located between the fledgling towns of Homestead and Florida City, which now border the perimeter of Everglades National Park. Long Glade was actually a "finger glade" that crossed the pine ridge to connect the Everglades with coastal prairies inland from Florida Bay and Biscayne Bay. Long Glade was one of many finger glades that allowed water to drain off the higher pinelands and hammocks and to drain eastward from the southeastern Everglades. The run-off water was channeled through these finger glades, also called transverse glades, toward the mangroves that fringe the small bays along Florida's southeastern coast. This fresh-water delivery system was crucial to the growth of the aquatic life that fed ducks, wading birds, otters, and alligators in the mangrove zone (Craighead 1964, 11). In 1914, John W. Harshberger, in a report for the Wagner Free Institute of Science, describes crossing the prairie and marshes south of Homestead, which at the time of his report extended

A rattlesnake caught by Glen in the Long Glade, 1944.

from the town of Cutler to where the Florida Keys break from the mainland. Harshberger specifically describes the geography and flora of the Florida City area—then called Detroit—which was directly adjacent to the Long Glade. Harshberger notes that "physiognomically, it resembles the Everglades. It is a vast saw-grass marsh in wet weather, or plain with open lagoons of water and intersected by numerous drainage channels. The tension line between the extreme southern pineland and the Great Coastal Prairie is not drawn sharply. The two formations sometimes blend imperceptibly" (1914, 178).

The evidence of contemporary life in South Florida has almost eradicated all traces of this breakaway section of the Everglades—where sawgrass marshes literally reached through the pinelands, skirting orchid-filled hammocks. Trailer parks, fast food restaurants, subdivisions, and acres of farmland now obscure this habitat that was once rich with panthers, rabbits, alligators, birds, and freshwater fish. Today when Glen travels the roads east of Everglades National Park, his eyes, now veiled with cataracts, urgently scan the horizon as he describes the changes that have occurred in the past eighty years. A slight dip in the road or depression within a tilled field reveal to Glen the sites of plowed-over gator holes, sloughs, and finger glades. Except for these subtle indicators, the Long Glade is lost from the landscape.

Miami's role as the epicenter of Florida's dramatic "land boom" of the 1920s has been well documented. Spurred by the relative economic prosperity of the 1920s, northeastern investors swarmed the Miami area searching for a lucrative piece of the Sunshine State. These newcomers, arriving on special chartered buses and trains, were immediately bombarded by real estate agents seeking prospective clients (George 1986, 35). This speculative assault was driven by massive advertising campaigns throughout the nation, leading some investors to buy Florida swampland sight unseen. By 1924, both the price of land and the number of building permits issued in Miami skyrocketed, ranking it well above other southern cities in real estate development (George 1986, 30). But this feeding frenzy of land speculation ended in the spring of 1926, leaving a paper trail of payment defaults and allegations of fraudulent land promotions. As Glen notes, those living in the glades country south of Miami were spared neither the fervor of land speculation nor the succeeding economic devastation.

The abrupt end of the Florida land boom in 1926 signaled the beginning of a profound economic depression for the state, impacting South Florida several years prior to the Great Depression, which gripped the rest of the country during the 1930s. In September 1926 a Category IV hurricane swept across South Florida, further crippling its unstable economy. Winds from this hurricane were recorded at 128 miles per hour, that is, before the anemometer perched atop Miami Beach's Alison Hospital was knocked out (Parks 1986, vi). More than one hundred Miami residents died in this storm, and the Red Cross estimated that thirteen hundred people in Miami were injured (Reardon 1926, 110). The

destruction was so widespread that the Florida East Coast Railway offered free passage to those wishing to flee the area (Parks 1986, vi).
While the damage was less severe in the glades country south of Miami,
the fields and groves of those struggling to farm around Homestead and
Florida City were severely flooded (Taylor, 163). A local historian describes the impact of the storm saying, "After the 1926 hurricane, the
community was so destitute that the age old barter system was revived
and the town workers were paid in script" (Taylor, 161). By 1928,
Homestead's two banks had closed their doors.

   Glen came of age during this bleak period in South Florida's history,
and he, as many of his contemporaries, turned to the land itself for survival. As Glen describes, the region's rich marshes provided locals with a
bounty of game and freshwater fish for subsistence. Small-scale farming
was feasible during the dry winter months on the finger glades and interior marshes within the current boundaries of the national park. In this
chapter, Glen's colorful vignettes offer a glimpse into the lives of those
who, while facing great economic uncertainties, first settled, raised chil-
dren, and forged communities along the marshes and pinelands of the
southern Everglades.

Hard Times

Oh, they say hard times are coming again,
I hope I'm gone if and when.
We was down to bone and skin,
And I don't want to go through that again.
We was so hungry, so skinny, and poor,
We only had the clothes we wore.
We'd jump in a gator hole next to shore,
And wash 'em on our ribcage, like a washboard.
Oh they say hard times are coming again,
I hope I'm gone if and when.
My skin hung down like moss on a log,
My hopes no higher than knuckles on a hog.
Daddy said we gonna sink or swim,
Eat'n swamp cabbage buds and muddy bream.

Chorus from "Hard Times," a song written by Glen Simmons

Some of this country's richest wildlife could be found in the Florida
City area before its settlement. Yet the men who experienced this wilderness first hand have died and left little or no written description of
this area's lost richness. Years ago, dozens of finger glades cut through
the rock lands. These glades in their virgin stage were the Everglades in
miniature: mostly sawgrass, willow-rimmed gator holes, virgin pines
along the edge of the glades, and hammock growth that was edged
with large palmettos. This area was filled with deep gator holes and
that's what raised the wildlife. Everything—bird, deer, otters, turtles,
alligators, and fish—thrive in and around a gator hole.[1] This stayed
pretty much that way until bulldozers come along in the 1940s. Mostly
west of Palm Hammock [Paradise Key], about ten of these finger glades
headed south and toward Biscayne and Florida Bay. Men spoke of
these glades by names and numbers, such as First Glade, Second Glade,
Twin Hammock Glade, and so on. Now that the gator holes, sloughs,
and inland glades have been filled-in, covered over with homes, high-
ways, and buildings [outside of the park's boundaries], the feeding
grounds for millions of wildlife are forever gone.

Long Glade, where we lived and grew up, was about five miles long, ran southeast and east, and came into Florida City from the northwest. Some places were one-quarter mile wide and some only a few hundred feet. When the water rose in the summer, a glade skiff could be pushed from one end of Long Glade to the other. You could stand on the edge of Long Glade, holler at night, and the echo would rebound off the virgin pines across the glade. When we were kids, it was all open glade, except we had to pull our boat over Mowry Street. The river went across at Mowry Street and there was a little bridge there, kind of a token bridge, to let the river through.[2] People used to fish there. The glade is still there, but it's filled-in in most places. They filled it in with rock and built homes on it, and what's left will eventually totally disappear.

The headwaters for this glade formed around Nixon Hammock. This was a big hammock, at least twenty-five acres.[3] A beautiful thing— but after the bulldozers came, the hammock got smaller each year. Long Glade emptied into a larger slough that I called the Wink Eye Slough since lots of its waters ended up in the Wink Eye Creek.[4] A slough is a hard thing to understand. It can be a mile wide in places, and all messed up with high places and low places and blind spots. Sloughs give the appearance of jumping around. From this slough, the water drained into many creeks, with Trout Creek being the main drain, and wound up in Manatee Bay and Long Sound, Snag Bay, and Joe Bay, and some flowed to Barnes Sound. The Wink Eye Slough came across where US 1 is now and started breaking up past the present Last Chance Saloon.[5] You can still see some of the depressions that were the old gator holes around this bar.

Locals called it the Wink Eye Creek because it seemed to be closed up until you got your boat into it—you used to hear that name, but I don't know who started it. But it was a good name. You had to sit low in the glade skiff for a hundred yards or more and pull yourself through a mangrove tunnel when coming into it from Snag Bay.[6] There were lots of little creeks in this area, but the Wink Eye Creek had two mouths, one heading into Snag Bay and the other going to Bay Sunday. The Wink Eye Creek was the only one of those waterways that had high land in it. About a mile and a half, or two miles, back from the bays there was some high land with some saw palmettos on it. We used to camp there.

Nowadays the water in some of these creeks is much lower, causing them to fill-in with buttonwoods and mangroves and absolutely disappear. I'd seen places where I'd catch snappers start to fill-up and open somewhere else. The early white men here traveling by glade skiffs kept these creeks open—they were criss-crossed with buttonwood logs. A friend, Argyle Hendry, used a saw to cut his way through the mangrove creeks, but most men used machetes. Some harder buttonwoods had to be sawed or ax-chopped the first time; then you could use a machete from then on. I'm probably the only man left that has traveled these small waterways, some of which I only traveled a few times. Generally, traveling these small waterways wasn't worth it because getting through them was much too much work.

The Wink Eye Slough was not a real productive place to hunt, although I used to see evidence of ancient Indians there when I was young. I found pot shards all up and down this old river. The old-timers used to go in there looking for something to eat or to sell—deer, gators, or crocodile—and some went in there to make moonshine. We'd keep it burned in places, and there was enough deer for people to hunt in the Wink Eye. We'd walk ahead of the boat a lot of times and drag it through the mangroves. I would just imagine if you tried to go into the Wink Eye now from Snag Bay, you'd have hell. That whole creek has probably grown plumb shut. Well, too much work and pain for what little you got out of it. Gators were not plentiful in the Wink Eye, and it took too much time getting from one passage to another. When hunting, we could get more in one night in some lakes or creeks than in two weeks in these mangroves. But I'm so glad that I went, and I hope no one ever regretted going with me. We would wind up with low wages, but I wish I was young enough to do it again.

A lot of these wide sloughs, like the Wink Eye, used to be lakes. I've measured the depth of every one of them sloughs with the iron rod I carried when gator hunting. Some of them were eight feet deep down to the rock. They had to have been a lake at one time or a big river that filled up with tidal mud, algae, and peat. It must have took thousands of years to level up. And as we crossed those areas, the rock came up to within a foot of the glade plane. This was where the lake ended.

There used to be many beautiful hammocks in the region around the Long Glade. One of those was Miller Hammock, named after someone who I think homesteaded there. Parts of the old Miller Hammock were still there when I was a kid. The Indians camped there in ancient times, and that's where the Florida City Trailer Park is now. Some of the oak trees are still there, most of the hammock is gone. It must have been about fifteen acres that bordered the river mouth on the north side and went along the margin of rock and glade.

There also used to be another big, beautiful hammock called Brewer Hammock. This hammock was a showy thing, and it came right up to the pinewoods. A bit of it's still there, but it's not as pretty and flamboyant as it used to be. You can see what's left of the Brewer Hammock if you look on the east side of the road that leads to the park [SR 9336], after it makes that big turn (called the Horse Head Corner), and you cross the first canal. A creek used to be where that canal is, and a little bit of that hammock is on the south side of that canal. The glade was deep there, in the middle of the pinewoods. Once in the wee hours of the morning, I was with my daddy driving along there and we saw old man Brewer sitting on a stump, just at daylight with a gun across his lap (this was about 1923). Daddy said, "He's waiting for a wildcat that's eating his chickens." Years later at old man Brewer's place I found some old car parts. I mean some old ones, like a copper headlight that burned kerosene. A few citrus trees still were growing there also, some key limes, some rangpur limes, and sour oranges too. Later the Corps of Army Engineers put a canal through the old homesite. The last thing to live there was the rangpur limes.

No doubt that most of the early hunters coming down from Cutler and Miami along the old Camp Jack Trail or by glade boat came for the game.[7] The Camp Jack Trail was the first road to come down through here. It was a wagon road to start and was never more than two ruts. Florida City was a very rich place for wildlife at that time. Signs of ancient people could be found along the margin of the pinelands and hammocks on the edge of the glade; now it's been plowed away. A lot of the Camp Jack Trail was still there when I was growing up. It crossed the Long Glade about a thousand feet from where we lived. Because the Long Glade was boggy, the trail was cross-laid with pine pole, and a wagon could wade across it on those cross lays. At the time, they weren't using the Camp Jack Trail as a main road anymore, but people still used it to get to their homesteads and hunting areas. So, with the cross-laying, they could just drive across it even if the water was high. When I was growing up, I would get those old logs out and bring them home to use in the wood stove. The pine hearts didn't rot, and they made good firewood.

The virgin gladeland down here was so boggy that a wagon or a horse couldn't run through it, only oxen. A mule couldn't stand up on it, unless it had muck shoes on. These muck shoes were made of iron, about a foot wide and a little over a foot long. They were flat, the front was round like a dinner plate, and there were holes in them so they wouldn't suck to the ground. If a mule didn't wear them muck shoes clamped down over his hooves, he'd sink way down in the virgin gladeland. Sometimes they'd sink three feet down before hitting the rock. Then he's stuck, and you can't get him out. I tell you, it's hell to get a mule out when he's stuck. I've seen men all around an old mad mule, pulling up one leg, then the other, trying to get him out of the glade. But after the glades had been farmed for a few years, they got hard enough for a mule to stand up on.

The first settlers who came down here set in to kill out all the gators they could. This was their recreation. They used to think that the alligators would get a baby or a dog. And they did get dogs. So they had to clean them out, I guess. They didn't sell 'em, just killed 'em. I heard that when they first started to put the road down to Flamingo in 1916 [Ingraham Highway], men rode down there on motorcycles on Saturdays and Sundays and would shoot gators from the road and leave them to rot. That was just the thing to do. It had to be done I guess, in order to settle here. At least that was the excuse they used for the slaughter. The local people skinned many of these gators that had been killed and left by Sunday hunters, and I did it as I was growing up—if we found them after they floated to the top of the water. But if the hide began to slip, they were worthless.[8] Bright sun will slip a gator in a hurry after it floats. It used to pay me to ramble the ditches and canals and skin the floaters that were killed by Sunday hunters. This killing still goes on.

Life on Long Glade

My mother bought two acres in 1916 along Long Glade. That was the year I was born. She saved enough money from what Daddy was making at the time. She was a very frugal woman. When she bought the land, it was at fifty dollars an acre. Soon after my mother's marriage in 1906, she and my daddy, James Simmons, went up Lostmans River in the Ten Thousand Islands and put up on an old Indian shell mound.[9] People used to farm on old Indian mounds, then they'd ship their produce by schooner to Key West. They had plenty of meat, curlews [white ibis], and other birds, but the armyworms eat up their crops. They didn't stay at Lostmans for very long as my daddy was always uneasy up there.[10]

Pa built our house out of rough lumber that they got from Frazier's sawmill. That house wasn't tied down, it stood up off the ground on some wooden blocks. I guess they just depended on its weight to keep it grounded. It was a one-room house, about sixteen to eighteen feet long and twelve feet wide. We all slept on cots in there and sat on boxes or a trunk. The kitchen was in the corner, and Ma cooked on a four-hole stove, which cost six dollars. Me and my middle brother, Alvin, sat on a trunk to eat at the table. That trunk had some long cracks in it. My brother knew just how to move so the crack would pinch my behind. He could look surprised when I hollered. In 1925, Pa finished off the unscreened porch and made it into another room.

About 1925, Pa said that for one time in his life he'd like to have a thousand dollars. During the land boom, Pa sold one of his acres on Long Glade (which he bought for fifty dollars) for thirteen hundred dollars to a man named B. W. Finley on credit. But my father made the mistake of giving him the deed, so we was never paid for the land. The land boom busted a year later, the year of the 1926 hurricane. That

*Glen's mother,
Maude Simmons,
1906.*

was his last hurricane as he was killed by a drunk driver two years later.

Finley never did give my mother any money. He said he didn't have it. He was a telegrapher. Before he moved next door to us, he'd go down to South America to get a job. He was a strange fellow. He built a house about twenty or thirty feet off the ground on stilts. He put a ladder up to that house when he wanted to go to sleep. He said there was no skeeters up there.

Course, the 1926 hurricane tore that house up—and he had a tin shed on the ground that was also wrecked. Finley also built a small

Glen's aunt, mother, and grandmother (from left) at Long Glade after the 1926 hurricane.

storm house out of cement block—it wasn't more than four or five feet high. We heard that the storm was coming on a radio that Finley built out of parts that he ordered. It was a squeaking, squawking thing. But he got a warning about the '26 storm on that thing. Before the storm, Daddy used to laugh about Finley's storm house. But when the storm came, Daddy was glad to get over there in it. We all sat in that thing on tomato crates as the storm went by. This was a long-lasting storm.

After the 1926 storm, several things happened. For the first time we had plenty of chicken to eat. Ours were all dead and scattered out, but good to eat. That's when us young'uns got something besides neck, feet, and legs. The storm also moved our house half into the glade. We never moved it back, just leveled it up a little. We had to tote water from the pitcher pump a little further, but we could catch bream off the porch.

*   *   *

Any boy fortunate enough to have grown up along these inland glades before too much settlement can remember romping barefoot, swinging from one willow tree to another, fishing, hunting, and working, toting logs on our shoulders for the wood stove, and rambling the trails and wagon roads. But even during hard times, the boys living along the glades and in Homestead were a hellish bunch.

Back about 1924, my oldest brother, Emmett, brought home a sambo mud fish [or bowfin, *Amia calva*]. Down on this end of the glades mud fish used to be plentiful. They are big old, black, ugly things. Now you don't hear much about them, and that's good. Well, they die slow out of water. My middle brother, Alvin, said, "Put your finger in his mouth, Glen." And the damn fool me did. Then the mud fish closed his mouth on my finger. Well, Pa heard me hollering and come a-running. He took a knife and pried the fish's mouth open. Then he said to Alvin, "Now put your finger in his mouth." Large saw palmettos and pines grew close to the house, and they soon covered my brother's escape. He didn't take time to say good-bye. He gave the mud fish time to die before returning home.

That middle brother, Alvin, didn't get outdone much, but one time I well remember when he was about nine years old, and I was six. He

Glen (front row, right) in the fourth grade at Homestead Elementary School, 1925.

and I were on a fishing trip, walking to some gator holes. He picked up a small gator about two and one-half feet long and toted him home. Ma met us at the door. Alvin held the gator behind him and said, "Guess what I got Ma!" She soon found out as the gator grabbed his behind and hung on. That done me a lot of good. Ma helped him get loose. A young gator has teeth as sharp as an ice pick.

I have a great appreciation for the worms not bothering the guava fruits during the Depression. For guavas were a big part of our intake in them days and grew wild around most everybody's house. We would have had to eat them guavas at night or ignore the worms entirely—as some do now. They weren't hand-planted either but planted by birds and kids. This brought on some dissension among the kids who commonly "claimed" trees and didn't want no one to take a guava without permission.

There was a family of Minorcans that had a fish and chicken market on the Dixie Highway, close to SW 4th Street [in Homestead]. This was a busy place during the winter, and there were lots of guava trees growing around it. The family's oldest boy, Buster Pacetti, was about ten years old at the time and had a hard time keeping kids out of his pet guava tree. So, he plugged the prettiest guava with some datil pepper and put the plug back in it while it was still hanging from the tree. Now there might be things hotter than datil pepper, but they are not on this earth. According to what Buster told us, his father bit into that guava. Buster was paddled with a barrel stave. This wasn't surprising since Buster was just trouble prone. He was run over by a wagon; he stuck an ice cleaver through his foot; he put one foot in a bucket of hot tar—all when he was very young.

*   *   *

A large sawmill was close by to our house. The large steam boiler was fired all night by the "fireman" so as to be ready for the 7 A.M. shift. Every engine and every tool was driven by steam power. This was a first class mill and covered several acres, even had a steam dry kiln and a steam whistle that everybody loved. Its steam whistle always blew on time and was the only clock anyone needed for miles around. At 6:45

A.M. the call whistle was sounded, two short blasts. At 7 A.M. one long blast and the carriage brought the first log to the saw. This went on all day until the long quitting whistle at five o'clock. I heard that that whistle blew a long time when World War I was over.

Many kids would come to the sawmill at night to play—this during the '20s. We were all over it—just romping around, playing games. One boy was killed when a stack of lumber fell on him. On one Halloween night in the mid–1920s some kid pulled the whistle wire at midnight, and it got hung up. It blew for several hours, screaming in the night. Every kid was in overdrive getting home. The fireman, so it was said, left too, and the owner of the mill who lived about a mile away had to get out of bed and come and turn off the whistle. The kids around our house sure didn't know nothing about no whistle blowing. No, no.

* * *

James Archer Smith came to Homestead about 1919 and never left. He had been a surgeon in World War I, so he pretty well knew his onions.[11] Everyone used him but not everyone paid him—including us. In 1921, I was sick with the measles. Ma walked the two miles to his office, and then he came rattling down the log road in a Model T Ford and waded the last hundred yards to the house. Being backwoodsy and not used to dressed-up people, I was uneasy. But Dr. Smith soon put me at ease. The thing I most remember was that when he was leaving, Dr. Smith gave me a nickel, and that was a nickel more than he got for the visit. Pa later give him his fee of a dollar.

Later on he saved my worthless hide, and that's when his army and war experience paid off. In 1929, I was with two fellows quail hunting. One of these fellow's folks had a grocery store and could afford a new Model A Ford. The Ford was a two-door sedan, and they let him drive it that day. We had found some fine King Oranges growing near an abandoned old homestead house. We put the oranges in the back seat of the Model A. Somehow or other, when I was reaching to the back seat from the running board a shotgun went off, and I was soon laying on the ground, shot from the knee to hip. I heard the gun go off, but didn't feel a thing. I remember saying, "What did you shoot?" Then I fell over. The boys put me on the running board. One boy drove the car, while the other held me on to the running board with his feet— as the owners' boy didn't want blood in the car. Thank goodness for

The pinewoods outside of Homestead in the early 1900s. Courtesy Arva Moore Parks.

running boards in them days. Now with these modern cars, there would have been no place for me to ride.

We went about three miles to the county hospital where Dr. Tower sewed the leg together somehow. Dr. Smith came in a little later and ripped the stitches out, saying it had to be left open to let out as much powder as possible. It was never sewn up again. Gangrene had set in, but Dr. Smith refused to cut my leg off. Fifty-eight days later, I went back home—that shack looked good.

Dr. Smith was well known for practical jokes. Many were true and no doubt many made up as happens after a fellow gets to be a legend. But one joke was told to me by a fellow that went on a fishing trip with the doctor. They were using a skiff with an outboard motor and were having no luck. The doc said something to the effect of "we got to have some fish if we're gonna have a fish fry. Hand me my tackle box, I got something to catch these fish with."

Well back in the '20s and '30s, dynamiting fish was quite common, although it was illegal then too. But you could buy dynamite then over the counter at Horn Hardware and Lumber Company. Even kids could buy dynamite. And, you know, we lived right next to a big magazine of dynamite. Wasn't over two or three hundred yards from us. If that thing had gone off, it would have blowed us slap into that Long Glade.

When fishing with dynamite, the older men would usually gather up us yearling boys and head to a canal looking for some fish to shoot. One of the best places was called the "big hole," and it was about a half mile from the mouth of the Florida City Canal where the canal spanned the Six Mile Creek. Here we could see that no one was ahead or behind us. If we used too much dynamite, it would break the fish's rib cage, and it'd kill too many. One and a half inches of dynamite was plenty—just enough to hold the cap. A hole a little bigger than the cap was punched in the dynamite and about two inches of fuse was teeth-crimped in the cap and shoved in the hole and packed with loose dynamite; a little dynamite was put on the end of the fuse so it would be easier to light. A match or glowing cigarette was used to light it. Us boys would stand around the canal with our clothes off. As soon as the charge was lit, thrown, and went off, we'd hit the water on the run. The fish would boil to the top, and the boys would throw them up out of the canal. The older men would sack them up. In five minutes, we would get out of there.

Now back to Doc Smith, he was sitting in the boat and had the charge all ready to go with the fuse in place. He lit the fuse, and as he threw it from the boat he hollered, "Watch out!" The dynamite had slipped out of his hand and rolled under the men's seat. Them fellows couldn't get overboard fast enough. They swam faster than any Olympic swimmer ever did. When they were about give out and out of the danger zone, they looked back and Doc was having a laughing fit. He'd pulled a good 'un with a piece of broomstick wrapped in dynamite paper.

Some of the land close in to town was farmed in the early years when 95 percent of the truck farming was done in the glades, this before bulldozers and irrigation. People farmed a lot of the gladeland even then. Since the farmers didn't have the equipment that they have now, they didn't clear the land entirely. Only since they came in here with drag lines could they level those gator holes with rock. People farmed in Long Glade, if the water went down. If they could plant by January, they'd plant those glades, and generally they'd have a dry enough spring to make a crop. These inland glades were known for being cold. They'd make pretty good crops in them times except they froze often. I remember when the millet was ready in the old farms, Pa and others would go hunting. They would all shoot across the fields at the same time with what they called "mustard seed," a very fine grade of shot. Then everyone would pick up the rice birds, a hundred or so, that they had killed.[12] All pitched in to pick the feathers and clean them. The birds were cooked with rice in a large pot, that was the "rollican" the old folks said. Some kind of good.

During the '20s and '30s, farmers would farm around the gator holes, and they plowed their fields with mules. You'd often see a gator trail right through the tomato field or the bean field, and you knew he was going to his hole or to visit a female. In the pineland, people would plant beans and things in the gator holes. They planted there because it was the easiest place to farm; there was dirt there. They would take a grubbing hoe and dig the holes in the clay pockets of the pinewoods and plant squash and tomatoes. Right in the pinewoods. That was in the fall of the year when there was some rainfall. It all depended upon the weather, whether they made a crop or not.

*　　*　　*

After my father was killed, the Depression was coming on, and we were without. Without him during the Depression, I realized how important he was. I tell people that we was so poor, we didn't even have roaches. But, even then, our Ma could make a meal out of nothing almost. She wore an apron when she would strike out down the glade, and there always would be something in the apron that she could make a meal out of when she got back. Sometimes she'd cook purslane—the crackers called it "puslet."[13] We ate guavas and coco plums that grew along the glade edge. And she'd make tea from the sweet bays in our yard. She'd also cook the wild pigeon peas that grew around the house. To make some money, she took in sewing from the black folks that lived around the sawmill. She would make fancy Sunday church clothes for the women. Mama charged them seventy-five cents to make a dress. Most sawmill laborers during the teens and '20s came from the Bahamas. They were doing better than most of the outlying whites as they were provided free housing and plenty of wood for their stoves. These Bahamians grew chickens, cassava, and pigeon peas. They fattened land crabs to eat by feeding them Spanish needles.

After Pa was killed in January of 1928, we really fell on hard times. A well-to-do neighbor had built not too far away—an old, retired farmer named Musselwhite. Sometime in the summer of 1929, he must have put fifty or more pumpkins in his yard to dry out. Now Ma was passing by and remarked to him, maybe she was hinting and hoping he might offer some pumpkins, but anyway she said, "You sure have some pretty pumpkins." "Yes," he said, "and you could too if you'd plant some seed." Well the pumpkins laid there until the '29 storm, the highest water we'd seen. A very wet storm. Pumpkins were floating everywhere. We could have give him some, but he didn't ask.

Aside from what our mother did, we did many things to get food. The Sullivan boys, who got stale bread from the bakery to feed their hogs, would throw some to us on their way to feed the hogs that they kept near the Smith Dairy.[14] When I was young, you used to see wild-cats everywhere. They could live around town, up close, because there were rabbits everywhere. My brother Emmett was a good rabbit hunter. He kept us in rabbits. Them days we also ate a lot of muddy fish that we caught in gator holes.

And if a person was not in such a hurry, enough food could be found around the gator holes, sloughs, and pinewoods to keep him alive. We pulled and ate thousands of silver palm buds and saw pal-mettos. The bud of the silver palm was better, and you quickly learned to pull out the two fronds next to the bud—that would loosen it. Cab-bage palm buds were not good along these glades since the woods burned often, which made the buds bitter. Beauty berries, gooseber-ries, and snow berries were everywhere, and coco plums were around the gator holes and richer soils. The pulp was eaten from the coco plums and the seed kept to be eaten later on. Sometimes we roasted the seeds in a frying pan. Guavas were around the vacant homesteads and farms and gator holes in the pinelands. Anywhere man rambled there were guavas, rangpur limes, key limes, sour oranges, and such. Some-time about August the wild persimmons would bear.

After the Land Boom

During the land boom here in South Florida, people went crazy to own some land. They were staking out subdivisions and building sidewalks all through the pinewoods. They'd said, "They'll be a home here and a home here," and they built roads through these pinewoods. That's all you could hear. The new sidewalks went way out east of Homestead. The Yankees were just buying it up, wanted to buy a little of South Florida. They were even buying up land in the middle of them Ever-glades, without even seeing it. They had such a rosy picture painted of South Florida that they bought it. I knew even old sawmill laborers who bought land down here in the Everglades. They didn't know what they were doing. Real estate agents would bring people on down from

Miami on buses to buy land, and they would stay at the Seminole Hotel in downtown Homestead—there being a fine restaurant there. Agents would stand on platforms selling land over loudspeakers to crowds of people gathered in front of the hotel. When the park came, the government officials found out that the land was owned by thousands of people.

The land boom dropped out after the 1926 hurricane, and it was rough going down here between 1927, '28, '29, and '30—and all the ways to the '40s. People were disillusioned and wouldn't, or couldn't, pay any taxes. It wasn't uncommon for houses and farmland to be sold for the taxes. But before the bust of 1926, people would put a little money down as a deposit and try to buy many parcels of land. Most of the land sales were only on paper.[15] So when the land boom ended, lots of people were overextended and went broke. I knew some of the real estate people who were very, very wealthy before the bust. And after that, they were out cooking in the yard. Everything they had was taken away from them because they owed so much money.

In 1925, Benjamin Morris, a real estate man who taught Sunday school, was so filthy rich on paper that he spent the whole Sunday School class period before Christmas writing checks for everyone in that class for twenty-five dollars—including me. I got a twenty-five dollar check. There were people that went to Sunday school that day that had never been—and some nearly voting age. He must have written a hundred checks. And they were good. But, they wouldn't have been good if you'd kept them awhile. Morris went under. He was walking, and he had nothing. They took everything he had. Before the land boom busted, he was called "boy wonder" and had a big write-up in the Miami papers.

About 1923 the Redland Road was put across Long Glade. It was a rock road at first, and there was a wooden bridge built over a large gator hole near our house. When they built that bridge, they sank a twenty-four-foot support plank down into the mud before hitting rock. Even then, the bridge still sank at one corner. In the fall, the water level would rise and wash across the road. The high water would bring fish and crawfish almost to our front steps. With a piece of sowbelly tied to a string or a baited screen, we'd soon have enough crawfish to cook or fish with. The fish and crawfish, in turn, attracted hundreds of night herons, what crackers called squawks. My older brother would stand on the road at night and shoot the herons for our dinner. After the land boom bottomed out, we were so poor that the cat was afraid to bring a rat home. Finally it got afraid to come home. Yet even then, we were happy when the water rose in the Long Glade and washed the mud out of the freshwater fish or when my brother Emmett brought home rabbits in one hand and a few stalks of sugarcane in the other.

*　　*　　*

In 1933 it was decided by the higher ups in Washington, D.C. to start the Civilian Conservation Corps. Young men could sign up for six-month hitches. They worked in the woods mainly. The pay was good for the times. You got thirty dollars a month, of which twenty-five dollars was sent home, and the rest, if there was any, was paid to the enlistee. If you came up short on your equipment, the amount would be taken out of your pay. I found out firsthand that a mess kit spoon was worth three cents. I joined in the first enlistment. Millions of young men did the same thing. Everyone lived in tents that I knew of. And after the first month of aggravation in Fort Benning, Georgia—getting all them shots and rough treatment when I was in the regular army years later—I can see why the regular army men didn't think it was right that the CCC boys got thirty dollars a month when they only got twenty-one dollars.

We came by train to the Ocala National Forest, then by truck to Crooked Lake where we set up camp. There was two hundred in each camp. Our camp had one hundred from the Tampa area and one hundred from Dade County. Five of us came from around Homestead, and we all lived in the same tent. A cone-shaped chunk burner was in the middle of the tent for heat. The ones in charge were a captain, a lieutenant, a mess sergeant, a buck sergeant, and a corporal. They kept order in a good fashion. This CCC camp had a few older men attached to it. The Depression had hit them hard. One that went with us was a civil engineer of about fifty years old. He taught us how to use a transit

Glen (back row, center) on a CCC surveying crew, Ocala National Forest, 1933.

and run a line. He had to stop and rest a lot. Cigarettes had about got him, as they did me later on.

I was fortunate enough to get in a surveying crew and stayed there. We went all over that government forest. During the workweek we surveyed the old section lines in the forest. I never felt so lucky to ramble that large track of wild land, day after day. So many lakes, ponds, creeks, and springs. It was great. A few of us spent a lot of weekends in the woods—walking, fishing, rambling, laying out. We found a one-room fishermen's camp with a wood stove and used it often. A small skiff was there, and we used it. I never tired of the woods.

Back at home, we did a lot of things to stretch our money during the lean years of the 1930s. For instance, I had a little outboard motor gas tank, which held a half gallon of gas, that I attached to my Model A Ford gas tank. I put kerosene in the main tank 'cause it was so cheap and ran that car on kerosene. I'd start it with gas and then switch tanks. It worked real well. And I saved twelve cents a gallon. You could buy five gallons of kerosene for forty-five cents from the Gulf plant.

Once I owed a gasoline bill for about twelve dollars. Lots of people in town owed a gas bill. So when this filling station bunch started building a motel, they hired all the people who owed a gas bill to work on it. The motel was made of a little bunch of cottages along the highway. I was paid two dollars a day, and they would keep a dollar of it and write it off your gas bill. And as soon as you got your bill paid up, they'd fire you. Then they'd hire someone else that owed them money.

You've got to live, and I didn't know any other way to live besides rambling around in the woods and hunting gators. I was doing better than any of my friends. At least I was making a living. Them poor fellows, they couldn't even put a down payment on a free lunch, most of them who went to school with me. I'll tell you, you would have to live back in them days to realize what the whole situation was.

Men could spend a week trying to get one day's work. I remember the county was hiring a few men on a one-day basis for two dollars a day, but I soon noticed that some were given more work than others. This was political, and I wasn't old enough to vote. Even as dumb as I was, I knew my fortune was somewhere else, if anywhere. The fellow in charge of hiring said it made him cry to turn me away, but I noticed that his friends always had a job. Maybe I was better off for it as gator hides had started to sell to some extent, and you could live in the glades for little or nothing.

It was great just being away from the roads. When in the glades away from the roads there was no prohi or game warden pawing through your lard-can suitcase or taking the spare tire apart.[16] Although hunting gators was as legal as preaching the gospel, the John Laws couldn't stand to think you might be in the woods. They no doubt had some help from jealous locals that weren't man enough to go in the glades on long trips. Now mind you this was before hunting with blow boats [airboats], blowflies [small planes], and glade buggies, and we never saw nobody. There was no park then; I owned it all.

Don't ever blame the people that were making a living from the land for the current scarcity of wildlife. Put the blame where it belongs—on development, government interference, and too many people. The Indians of yesterdays hunted the year around and destroyed nothing. When a road is built to replace a trail, the woods are not the same anymore. It's all over, folks.

Everglades
Backcountry Camps

For a century, the financial promise of exotic plume feathers, gator hides, and otter and raccoon pelts lured generations of hunters deep into the rugged Everglades backcountry. On these trips, it was common for gladesmen to remain in the remote backcountry for weeks and even months at a time—setting up temporary camps on hardwood hammocks or beneath the tangled mangroves along a coastal river. Yet Glen Simmons notes that before the 1940s, it was exceedingly rare for him to meet anyone else except for an occasional moonshiner or Seminole Indian during his hunting and camping trips into the interior swamps. While the region consistently offered the few men who braved its environs ample resources for survival, Glen's descriptions of backcountry life suggest how arduous and isolating these trips could be.

Glen, at the age of fourteen, began accompanying much older men into the Everglades for lengthy periods. From these men—Argyle Hendry, Buck Rohrer, Ed Brooker, Lige Powers, and others—he learned the skills necessary for survival in the Everglades backcountry. Both the material culture and hunting techniques used by Glen (such as burning the glades to attract game) appear not to have substantially differed from those used by the men who lived and hunted in the Everglades during the nineteenth century. Glen's experiences therefore represent an important link to, and continuation of, the cultural practices of an earlier era.

South Florida essentially experiences only two seasons: rainy and dry. The rainy season—with its characteristic afternoon rains, sudden thunderstorms, and hurricanes—begins in the early summer and lasts until fall. Then the glades and mangrove swamps become flooded from horizon to horizon. The winter and early spring months, however, bring blue skies and dramatically lower water levels and except for the deeper sloughs, ponds, and tidal areas, much of the country becomes dry. In many places, the marsh becomes so parched that the periphyton algal mats dehydrate, leaving an almost white, crusty film—called "snow" by early setters—over the marsh's surface soils.

Gladesmen adapted to these dramatically different seasons both in their means of traveling the glades and in their choice of prey. During the rainy season, light, flat-bottomed boats called "glade skiffs" were used to negotiate the shallow waters of South Florida's "river of grass." During the dry season gladesmen walked into the glades, carrying all their supplies in burlap sacks (what Glen refers to as "walk-hunting" or "pole-hunting"). After the first part of the Ingraham Highway was completed in 1916 (which eventually connected Homestead to Cape Sable), moonshiners and hunters began using this road as their main departure point into the Everglades.[1] Gladesmen were either dropped off along the Ingraham Highway, also called the Cape Sable Road, or they hid their cars in the brush along the road before heading to their camps hidden on mangrove islands and hardwood hammocks.

Bringing a minimum of supplies with them, gladesmen necessarily relied upon their own resourcefulness for the basics: food, fresh water, and shelter from storms and wet ground. According to Glen, essentials that were taken on every trip included mosquito netting (called skeeter bars), a ground cover, rifles, ammunition, tobacco, a pocketknife, a machete, salt, coffee, meat (usually that had been cooked down and stored in

Cast-iron cookware and a lard-can suitcase at a North River camp, 1938.

lard), matches, and cooking grease. If traveling by boat, gladesmen would carry along fresh water, although rarely enough to last an entire trip. Finding fresh water could be difficult, particularly during the spring months when water levels were lowest or along the coastal areas where saline content was often high. When fresh water was scarce, brackish water was used for cooking, or occasionally stills were carried for desalinization purposes. To discourage mosquitoes, gladesmen typically kept smoldering fires of black mangrove burning at all times. These "smokes" were the first thing attended to in the morning and were kept burning throughout the day—often even in smudge pots within their boats. Each gladesman had his own favorite base camps where canned goods (such as cooked-down meat) were buried and supplies (such as dry wood or a change of clothes) were stored in tin lard cans purchased in town.

Regardless of whether they were walking or using boats, the men who hunted and camped the southern Everglades traditionally stuck to standard routes. These routes, or trails, often amounted to a system of watery passages through the thick tangles of mangroves separating the various lakes and ponds. Often these routes had to be recleared each season and were thus "rediscovered" after observing the direction of the water flow between the mangroves and by detecting signs of prior usage. Frank Chapman, curator of the American Museum of Natural History, traveled along one of these routes to the famed Cuthbert Rookery in March of 1908—guided by locals Melch Roberts and Louis Bradley. Because it was a favorite spot for plume hunters, the route to Cuthbert was fairly well traveled. Yet as Chapman describes, even the well-traveled routes were difficult to navigate: "For four hours we followed channels through the mangroves, often so narrow that there was barely room for the passage of the boats. The branches formed a dense canopy overhead, and marks of the ax showed they had grown as freely below, in places, limbs and roots having been cut out every yard of the way" (1908, 140). Almost twenty years later, Van Campen Heilner took a similar route to the Cuthbert Rookery and, although plume hunters had visited this rookery on several prior occasions, he seemed equally startled by its inaccessibility and abundance of wildlife (1922, 135). Several of these routes crossed the Ingraham Highway and were as well known to these backcountry woodsmen as are the popular intersections in any town. These "jumping-off" points or "landings" were marked by subtle variations in the landscape (a solitary palm, for instance) and were often named after the person who "claimed" the route (for instance, Ed Brooker's Landing). Two of the routes Glen discusses, the "Reef" and the "Interior Route" (also called the Eastern Creek Route), served as principle corridors across the southern Everglades for "glade skiffers." Today, a number of these established routes, such as the Hell's Bay Trail and the Noble Hammock Canoe Trail, are maintained by the National Park Service.

In describing the actual landscape of the region, Glen recalls the common place-names locals used before the establishment of the national park—the names of popular camps, of sloughs, and of regions within the mangrove island–filled backcountry. For the gladesman, these place-names served as important mnemonic devices for navigating the vast expanse of wilderness that is the Everglades. Without maps, Glen and his contemporaries used these sites as anchoring devices within the complex system of watery terrain where they spent the majority of their time. For instance, a gladesman would know that it would take a day to pole, heading westerly, from Ed Brooker's Camp to Seven Mile Camp along what was then called the "Reef" country. Each of these colorful names—the "Bill Ashley Jungles," for instance—refer to a story or incident known only to this small community. Moreover, the stories linked to these camps served to instill a sense of community and common history within a network of men who literally spent weeks at a time in complete isolation in the middle of the Everglades.

Before the advent of airboats, South Florida gladesmen used shallow, flat-bottomed skiffs to travel the Everglades backcountry. These hand-crafted glade skiffs represented by far the most practical mode of Everglades transportation, providing gladesmen with equal access to the narrow passages within the mangrove swamps, the shallow waters of the sawgrass marshes, and the open expanses of Florida Bay. Camps were

Glade skiffs at a surveyors' camp on Cape Sable, circa 1920.

A Seminole dugout canoe, late 1930s. Courtesy Alexander Sprunt IV.

primarily located next to skiff-accessible waterways—scattered along glade skiff trails and canal banks and around various backcountry ponds and lakes. The camps' positions, as shown on the map in the preface, suggest the importance of the skiff to glades culture.

Although less common, some locals, including Glen, also used Seminole dugout canoes in the Everglades. The two boats are fairly similar, although skiffs were usually much shorter and lighter than dugouts. Glen describes the difference in the boats saying, "Them with the dugouts could carry the whole family. But when you got in tight trails [in the mangroves], where you had to turn a lot, you didn't want that dugout. You should try turning that thing. When you were in open glades [in a dugout], you could just go. Just work out them sloughs."

Gladesmen regularly poled their skiffs for days on end, an activity that often involved hacking and shoving through walls of mangrove as well as fighting the wind and currents in open waters. On the more infrequently traveled routes, as Glen describes, lying down in the boat and pulling it under the tight spots was generally the best course of action. With this in mind, Col. Hugh Willoughby's assertion that skillful poling was an "absolute" necessity for work in the Everglades seems hardly an understatement (1898, 37).

The bow of a skiff loaded with camping gear near the Reef north of Taylor Creek, 1934.

To achieve their maneuverability, skiffs were fairly narrow, usually about two feet wide. Generally sixteen to eighteen feet in length, skiffs had to be long enough to accommodate the amount of gear (sometimes for two men) needed on multiweek trips into the backcountry. To make poling the boats easier, skeeter bars, lard-can suitcases, cooking pots, guns, and alligator hides had to be carefully balanced within the boat.

Boat poles were typically fifteen feet long and made of local cypress. A forked foot at the pole's end prevented it from sinking too far into the region's soft muck—which would break the poler's stride. Glen affixes a thick piece of rubber, often from a tire, to the pole's foot. This makes poling much quieter, preventing the sound the pole makes when it hits rocks along the bottom from spooking game. The poler usually stands toward the back of the boat, elevated above the glade plane on a poling platform. From this position, the poler can watch the bottom for signs of game as well as monitor changes in the surrounding landscape. While poling a boat all day in the hot, buggy Everglades is by no means easy, it requires much less energy than paddling a comparable distance. For instance, in open water Glen is able to push the skiff almost one hundred yards with one stroke, making it possible to "pole all day" without tiring.

Traditionally, the skiff's wedge-shaped bow was formed by the intersection of two cypress boards. This wedged bow allowed the poler to part and glide over the Everglades' thick, grassy waters. A five-inch lift built into the skiff's stern made this process almost silent, as the lift prevented the bow from slapping against the water. The stern's updraft also allowed the skiff to be poled stern first, granting the poler greater maneuverability when turning around in narrow passages proved impractical. As the skiff's bottom was utterly flat, the poler could travel across miles of shallow marshes where the water was often only inches deep.

Glen building a sixteen-foot skiff, 1934.

Glen began building skiffs at the age of twelve. He explains how he began building these boats by saying, "When you're growing up in a country and see all the men with glade skiffs, you knew you wanted to build one. They were a simple boat, just wedge shaped. But you took pride in them, the way they looked." Early skiffs were made out of locally milled cypress boards, and they needed to be kept in the water to prevent them from leaking. Occasionally the bottoms of the boats were planked with tomato field crates made of cypress. When the cypress skiffs dried out, it was necessary to soak them for a number of days until the boards swelled again. If the boats were needed sooner than the soaking period would allow, Glen advises that "the best and quickest way to ready them was to use Octagon soap. Just rub that yellow soap across the cracks, and in short order she'd float high and dry, and blow bubbles as she went along. Pushing out the soap as she swelled."

As cypress became scarce during the war years, Glen began to substitute marine plywood for the skiff's bow and bottom. His unique construction technique involves soaking, bending, and suturing a split piece of marine plywood to form the bow. He continues to use cypress for the sides and stern of the skiff. The appendix includes specific instructions for building a glade skiff based upon Glen's design.

The use of glade skiffs began to wane during the 1940s as airboats (flat-bottomed crafts propelled by an airplane engine) gained popularity. Glen remains one of the last builders of the Florida glade skiff, and his boats are currently on permanent display at the State Folklife Museum in White Springs, Florida, and at the Historical Museum of Southern Florida in Miami. Glen has been recognized by the State of Florida, through a Florida Heritage Award, for his skiff-building expertise.

Camps in the Everglades

Years before the park was established, when all the land and marsh seemed to belong to me, we would help ourselves to whatever we could sell or trade for survival. Mostly we would sell gator and otter hides to different buyers. Before the park, men had camps all over this country. There must have been a hundred of these camps that we used when gator hunting. A camp could be in a hammock or just a hole hollowed out; usually it was just a piece of higher ground that had been cleared. Most of these camps were just drift camps, places where the peat had settled and formed a small mound and a hammock would get started — many times from a gator nest. Rarely did any of our camps have any

Glen's self-portrait at the Madeira Farms Camp, 1934. He's holding the string on the camera timer.

kind of permanent structure on them. A lot of these old camps had pot shards on them, especially the camps that were along the edge of a slough. The Indians must have used them over five hundred years before we did.

All these camps had names. They were either named after something that had happened at that spot or named after how far they were from the road (such as the East Seven Mile Camp, or the West Seven Mile Camp). Others were named for someone who camped at the site or after a lake or a creek. There was Camp Nasty (more were known by the name of Camp Nasty, maybe, than any other), Oak Trees, Doe Head Camp, Little Banana Patch, Kettle Camp, Hendry, Barber, Wet Hammock, Reef Camp, Sloan's Monument Camp, Black Hammock, Hog Back, Rat Camp, Break-A-Leg, Quarles Camp, Broken Bones, Buzzard, and Radius Rod. The names went on and on. The people

A skeeter bar with tarpaulin covering at Cuthbert Lake, late 1930s. Leaves and branches are draped over the skeeter bar to help keep the bar cool.

who spent time in these glades, hammocks, and mangroves all knew the names of the camps. Now most of the camps have been burned away completely—especially the ones made on peat. The fires during the extremely dry spring of 1934 and in 1962 caused many campgrounds to burn down to the rock.

If we were glade skiffing, we always carried a skeeter bar with us to sleep under. Skeeter bars were homemade, any size you wanted, made out of cheesecloth or sugar sacks sewed together. A bar 4' x 6.5' x 3' was mostly what we used. We attached the skeeter bar to the tarpaulin—about three feet off the ground. The sides of the skeeter bar hung down and was tucked under your bedding. We used our guns, or shoes, or a blanket to hold the sides of the skeeter bar down and away so it wouldn't billow in. Anything to bar the skeeters.

When we got to a camp, we would gather up grass (switch grass or bunch grass and sawgrass) and pile it up for bedding. I called these piles "gator-nest beds." Sometimes we actually flattened out real gator nests for beds and camps, but generally they were full of ants after the gator eggs hatched. You could hide your supplies at a camp and use it as a base for hunting the area. I'd often bury a jar full of cooked-down meat packed in lard at one of my camps. We'd also keep a few canned goods at our camps. But even though we rarely met anyone on these trips, we had to hide our supplies. If not, hellish people would steal or disturb anything they found hidden at a camp.

Making Burns in the Bill Ashley Jungles

The Bill Ashley Jungles was a big area and it formed the headwaters of the East River. If you could see all the creeks that made up the headwaters of the East River from above, it would look like the tangled roots of a very large old tree. These so-called jungles are mangrove, buttonwood, mahogany, and bustic—all the plants found on high land except pine. The jungles was full of game and birds. I used to go there with Ed Brooker, or with other men, from 1929 to 1939—and a few scattered trips later on.

In the Bill Ashley Jungles, men would burn off the clumps of high ground that stuck out about two feet above the water to make feed.[2]

Some of these clumps would be fifty feet across. Burning also made traveling easier for men since it marked the trail. All the deer hunters made burns—it made the deer more plentiful and fatter. These burns made the glades so rich, when people asked me how I was doing I'd sometimes answer "burnt woods." You set dried paurotis palm leaves or palmettos afire to save matches when making the burns. All of the southern glades were burned in patches to the extent that the fire would go out when it reached a recent burn. There were burns of different ages all over the glades. Areas wouldn't burn for at least another year. But a lot couldn't burn again for a couple of years.

Most men went into the woods in the winter and fall. Then the hammocks and the peat would be wet enough so that they wouldn't burn out. In the rocky glades, you could walk for days, burning the clumps as you went along. If the water was high, and we was hunting from skiffs, we'd still burn as we went along. This marked the trail.

We mostly burnt when things were wet. In the rainy season, you just waited till it stopped. Most burns were small. They'd burn for ten minutes to two hours. But some hunters just made burns all the time. The Indians too. The water [rain] around here can cut off in October, then you might not see rain again for six months—except for a little trickling rain now and then. Then things can get pretty dry. Then the burns can get out of hand. Some people are just bad to burn.

In the mangroves you could burn anytime, as mostly the clumps would burn [areas of scattered mangroves in marsh, like parts of the Bill Ashley Jungles]. Burn everything you came to. You could burn all year round in the mangrove country without too much damage. Though I have seen a lot burned away—it burned bad back behind Little Madeira Bay once. There's not much variation in the water in the mangroves (only about a foot because of the tidal influence). A man might set twenty or more clumps a day on fire. We'd burn in the mangroves so we'd recognize where we'd been. Deer would take to the burns right away. A few days after this riverhead country is burned, the deer would pull the sawgrass buds and eat the tender white part. (They were good to man also, raw or cooked with bacon, I've eat thousands.) I never saw this happen anywhere except in the mangrove jungles. But you could tell a new burn there by the many white buds that had been pulled. These burns kept the sawgrass less heavy. Nothing thrives in thick sawgrass—save a few lizards, frogs, and snails. Deer and birds would get much thicker when you burned.

In the early days, before they put the canals and roads in down here, the glades rarely got dry enough to cause any bad fires—except along the edges. No doubt these edges burned out, when there was no roads or canals to stop the spread of the fire. There was a very bad fire down here in 1902 that started that way. After drainage, the glades were in danger of bad burnout during the late spring and were subject to "burn to the bone"—when the peat would burn down all the way to the rock. Burning when the peat was wet in the fall was the only sensible answer—this kept the buildup from getting too bad. For the most part the hammocks were still there when the park came. About 75 percent of them have now been burned out completely—too much tinder buildup caused some really hot fires. Now when there's a flood there's no place for animals to take refuge. The drowning of animals now are owed to the government. I have lived long and seen much and shed a few tears at the mess that has been made.

The Reef Country

The Reef crosses the Bill Ashley Jungles, and otters and birds would come to the Reef because there was more water here.[3] Ed Brooker explained how the Reef worked to me. This name was used by the surveyors in 1925 when they were working from glade skiffs. For ten years or more you could see the initials of the surveyors, which were carved in a sweet bay tree there (at the Seven Mile Camp east of the landings). I picked up the term from Ed Brooker, and everyone used it to locate a place when talking of an area. As for instance, one might say that he camped near the Reef north of Seven Palm Lake. If you was to see the Reef Trail today, you would swear no man had ever been there. But after the canal and road was cut across the East River head-waters in 1916 [Ingraham Highway and canal], men began hanging out in there. They, traveling in glade skiffs and whiskey scows, cut out these grown-over creeks—just wide enough to get through.

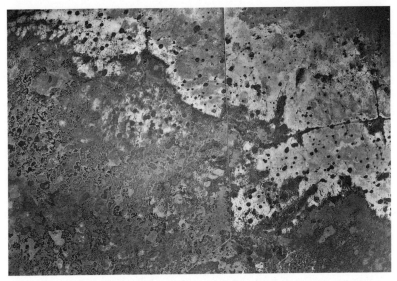

Aerial photograph showing the old Ingraham Highway heading south, then turning southwest to Flamingo, 1940. The Reef crosses the road at Whiskey Creek and is distinguished by the band of lighter color. Courtesy Everglades National Park.

The Reef country is about a half mile wide, on average, and is peat. It ran along the marl gladeland. The peat was of a slightly higher elevation than the glades that come to it. When traveling along the Reef, you stayed just outside of it. 'Cause the water was deeper. [The Reef Trail, which runs along the outside of the Reef, as shown on the map, crosses the old Ingraham Highway at Whiskey Creek and continues both east and west from the road.] The Reef begins to loose its character, breaking up and such, after it crosses the Taylor Slough. From there on, to the east, it wasn't that well defined. But the water along the Reef Trail was still a little deeper there than the glade.

Along the river headwaters there are thousands of small rock holes in the Reef. I also called this area the "margin," as it is where the marl and the peat meet. As the water was much deeper here, all glade skiff travelers used it, and it was ripe with fish, deer, and birds. The Reef is erratic, dotted with ponds, mangroves, and hammock growth. Now if your boat pole gets hung up in one of those holes, as they oftentimes did, well you'd better turn it loose and wade back to get it. If you held onto it, it would often snap off, and then you'd be in a real mess. This happened plenty.

We made these early poles out of cypress rounds of one inch in diameter. They usually were fourteen to sixteen feet long with a shoe, or a small forked divide, on the end to help keep it from going too deep into the mud. And if you think the shoe don't help, just try it without it.

On one occasion when my pole got hung up, I stepped overboard in about two feet of water. I thought I would stop the boat and wade back and get the pole. Umm ba ha! My right foot slid in a rock hole, and I let out a holler from the pain, but there was nobody but me to hear for miles. Then my foot wouldn't come out. I tried to work it out easily, at first, but I could tell it wasn't moving so I decided I had to get it out before it swelled up. I figured out how it went in and knew it had to come out that way. I even thought of putting the .22 rifle under the water to shoot out the rock. We often shot gators that way when we were in a hurry and couldn't get them to rise. However, the boat and the gun were out of reach, and I would have probably shot my foot off anyway. I was desperate at this point and knew that if it swelled up, I might be stuck there till death do us part. I remember laughing and maybe a little crying all at the same time. I stood there for about thirty minutes when I finally made my left, bare foot crawl around until things seemed to line up best in the hole. Then I used all the force I could muster and fell backwards, hollering. That bloody foot came out. I just lay there in the water as happy as I had ever been. Now sixty years later, no matter how bad I feel if I can just think of two things I usually feel better. One is that I ain't in the army and the other is my foot ain't hung in a rock hole. That experience was so bad I considered wearing shoes. Instead, I just stopped going overboard when the pole hung and just turned it loose and poled or paddled back with the .22 rifle.

Camping with Ed Brooker in the Bill Ashley Jungles

Down at Ed Brooker's camp, where we used to go, the trails was kept open by a few old timers. This camp was at the headwaters of the East River in the Bill Ashley Jungles, but you can't get through there now unless you do a lot of chopping.[4] You certainly couldn't get a glade skiff through there since some of the passageways are so narrow. We'd come through the Bill Ashley Jungles by a glade boat to Ed Brooker's Camp—maybe half a mile of crooks and turns from the road. There was a landing at the Ingraham Highway where a trail traveled east and west. From there, a mangrove tunnel led back into the country behind Seven Palm Lake. Ed Brooker always killed a few gators back there. There was a lot of deer near Ed Brooker's camp, and he could kill a deer a week, if needed. Ed would bring the hindquarters into town and trade them with his old-time friends for supplies. Ed came down here in 1904 and had hunted otter and plumes around Lake Okeechobee before that. There are lakes named after him and his brothers around Lake Okeechobee. Ed was a prominent man for awhile. He was the first railroad agent in Homestead and had a store in Florida City (then called Detroit). My family lived on a piece of land he had homesteaded; my folks lived there in 1913.

But, I tell you, Ed really worked that mangrove swamp—kept it burned in patches like he was farming for deer. He camped on and off at that spot beginning in 1916 when the road was first put there. But in the '30s, during the Depression, he stayed in there a lot. A black fella stayed in the camp with him and cooked. He was freckle-faced and went by the name of "Red." I give him a pair of WPA britches one time, and he was thankful for that. The cook had evidently got into some trouble making whiskey at one time. The law let him come down there and live in the woods with Ed, I was told. Red used a glade skiff to clear those islands, and he planted tomatoes and beans. But he only cleared the centers of the hammocks, leaving the outside intact. This way his farmed plots would remain hidden from people passing by— and Ed could also slip up on a deer that was eating his beans. They lived on deer meat and whatever they could plant. Ed would bring me a few gator hides. Later on he would get my wife to read his horoscope to him from the newspaper—as he was about blind.

*　*　*

There used to be many trails cut out all through the Bill Ashley Jungles. When the canal and road was dug across the East River headwaters about 1916, men began hanging out there. It became a fair country for gators, otters, deer, birds, fish, and moonshine. Perfect for skeeters, deerflies, and prohibition officers. They, traveling in glade skiffs and whiskey scows, cut out these grown-over creeks—just wide enough to fit through. Early white man cut trails that would allow a two-foot-wide glade skiff to get through. Those within a half mile of the road were wide enough for a whiskey scow of four feet wide to go and come (as most stills were within a half mile of the road). These waterways, if you could call them that, have grown plumb shut with mangroves over the years.

Once at night when I was hunting this country with Ed Brooker—him sitting on the seat feeling for a gator he'd shot and me poling—we got turned around. After he pulled the gator in the boat, he pointed to an opening in the bushes. I said, "That's the way we come." Now he started using some of the same words as a mullet fisherman does when he gets a net full of catfish. He accused me of turning the boat around and getting him lost. When we started off that night fire-hunting on some of his known trails, Ed said, "I'll show you that I know my onions."[5] Maybe that's why he threw such a fit when he got "turned around." But after awhile and after a lot of useless poling, he straightened it out. There's a lot of ways to go, but only one way goes through generally.

*　*　*

As I said, Ed Brooker was a prominent man when he was younger. But the moonshine got tasting better to him all the time, and he lost it all. In the '20s and '30s, he was hanging out in the Bill Ashley Jungles, barely getting by. Ed would pick up a fellow to take with him for a week or so at a time—or till the moonshine run out. But generally, he knew where a still was. To go out with him when I was a boy was great, at least to me. It seems that if he had moonshine, he could work all day and half the night pushing and pulling the glade skiff. He knew every hole where there might be a gator and could travel this rough country by night. When ready to go to town, he'd kill a deer and trade it to his old well-to-do cronies for grub and grog.

I'm thankful for the times I spent with him, but something happened on one trip that ended my trips with him. This was about 1934. We was coming from the north, heading to the country behind Cuthbert and Seven Palm Lakes, planning to stay a week. But Ed was already low on 'shine and had been known to head back when he was running low. We were poling along the freshwater Reef, when we saw a whiskey scow heading toward the landing [about a quarter of a mile east of the Ingraham Highway]. Ed poled us over to the scow, as we both knew the man. He was a friend of mine and said he was heading back to town to get some sugar to sweeten-up with [add sugar to the moonshine buck]. Right away, this man accused Ed of turning up his still. They got into a fuss. Ed swore it wasn't so, and he wanted 'shine. So after they both cooled off a little, we was told to follow his trail back to the still. The still was about a half mile from the Ingraham Highway, east of where Nine Mile Pond is now.

When we got close to the still, Ed hollered—telling those boys who we was and what we wanted. The three men at the still were uneasy and sullen. We knew them. I assured them that they had nothing to fear from me. And as long as I've lived, nothing by me was ever mentioned or no names. Well, Ed was given some backings, called low wines. These low wines are very harsh tasting, they don't proof out much. Too low to drink. I've been told a man shouldn't drink it, but Ed did, and there was hell to pay. Even Ed couldn't handle it.

The weather was hot and rainy, and the skeeters were some kind of bad. In two days we made our way to Cuthbert and Seven Palm Lakes. Ed had been drinking the low wines and chasing it with swamp water that was a little brackish and stinking—as the heavy rains had drowned all the wiggle tails, and they had swelled up by the millions. Ed was sick and cramping bad. He got to moaning and groaning and had the squirts bad. We made a quick-camp on a clump at dark. We built some smokes, but the rain put them out. Seems like every few minutes, Ed would run out of the skeeter bar, jump on the stern of the boat, drop his pants, grunt and groan, with the skeeters tar-black thick, and then back he'd come. Each time, letting a thousand skeeters into the bar.

About the third time of Ed coming under the skeeter bar, he said that he'd be damned if he was going out there again. He said if he had to mess again, he'd dig a hole at the foot of the bar. He was told that if he did such a trick as that, I'd made my last trip with him. After awhile, I heard him digging a hole. I never went with him again. Anyhow, he quit drinking out of that jug. He did much better for the next few days. On the way back, we stopped by the still again. The 'shiners had left. The still was gone, and the forty or fifty oak barrels had been put overboard to keep swelled. They couldn't take any chance of the news getting out. I never visited that site again. But please don't think that Ed had anything to do with turning up that still. He liked to drink too much.

*   *   *

Once while hunting with Ed Brooker in the Bill Ashley Jungles, I noticed some mahogany growing on the small islands. This was about 1934. I found a fella who said he wanted the wood for making furniture.

It was summertime and the skeeters, deerflies, heat, and rain were particularly bad. I had talked a young Samson of a man into going with me on equal shares to get the mahogany logs out of the jungles. We went by glade boat and camped on Brooker's Island. As we traveled from island to island, we cut the logs we could handle with a crosscut saw. Seems like some of these gladeland islands were fairly high with hard-packed peat floors.

The skeeters were so thick we had to keep the smudge fires smoking while we worked. That young bull of a man could "end over end" the eight-foot logs to the water. Once to the water, I would push and pull the loaded skiff through the shallow water to the road. The skiff could only carry one log or two smaller ones at a time and the road was about three-quarters of a mile from where we were working. None of these logs were over a foot in diameter. We then were able to carry the logs into town on the back of a cut-down Model A and take them directly to Jeffrey's Mill.

Since this method was so slow, I talked a moonshiner into lending me his whiskey scow. These bargelike boats used by moonshiners could carry a ton of sugar and much more mahogany than my glade skiff. He agreed, although he said I had to wait until nine A.M. on the following day since he was using the scow until then to haul supplies to his still. His operation was to the east and across the road from where we were working. The next morning, as I had no watch, I guessed at the time of day by gauging the time it took to drive the twenty-five miles from Homestead. The moonshiner's scow was supposed to be hidden in a shrouded mangrove cove along the road. I hadn't told the big Yankee strong man, who was helping me, about the moonshiner. I drove the Model A about a hundred feet past the place where the scow was supposed to be hidden and walked back up the road. Mr. Muscle stayed in the Model A. The boat was under a large overhang of mangroves, totally hid from the road. I ducked under the mangroves and was surprised to see that the boat was loaded with demijohns of 'shine and three men. I was a little worried when I saw them, as I knew they had been watching me through the mangroves. Assuring them they had nothing to worry about from me, I left and drove up the road a ways. After a half an hour, I saw a black fish truck pass and knew the coast was clear. We went back and pulled the scow across the rock road on some small log rollers that Ed Brooker kept hid behind the bushes to move his glade skiff from one side of the road to the other.

We were able to get most of the cut mahogany to the road by dark. My partner at this point had had enough of the heat, rain, skeeters, deer flies, and pulling and pushing that loaded scow through mangrove trails, which were not large enough to accommodate a four-foot-wide boat. It was as close to hell as a man wants to get—but at least I was used to it. I had never made an easy dollar anyway. My partner, on the other hand, said in harsh language, "If you take me into town right now, you can have the (blank, blank) mahogany!" We put the scow back in its hiding place and left for town. I never did see him again; I think he had enough of the great outdoors. I sold the wood on credit, which, if I had gotten paid, would have been worth about eighty dollars. A lot of money in the early 1930s. But the fella only ever paid me enough to cover the cost of the milling. I never got any more. If it hadn't been for a few gators I got on the trip, it would have been bad.

Moonshiners in the Bill Ashley Jungles

On another trip in 1932, I was camped a mile or so westerly in the Bill Ashley Jungles. This camping spot was the main landing—as the Ingraham Highway crossed Whiskey Creek there. You could come or go from this landing easterly or westerly. I went in by glade skiff with Ira Davis. The trails in there are barely wide enough to pole your skiff, and they branch out in every direction. Unfortunately, only one direction usually goes through, and you'd better take the right one or have plenty of time and energy. A light rain started to fall during the late morning, and the sky became overhung and darkish. We were heading west that day toward the Seven Mile Camp near the East River bird rookery. This trail was very ragged, and we lost our direction, sometimes finding the trail only to lose it again. This went on all day so just before nightfall, with the rain still falling lightly, we decided to spend the night on a clump.

We turned the boat over and tried to get a fire started underneath it. Everything was wet, and we had nothing to eat as we expected to be in camp by dark. You can pull the lead from a .22 bullet with your teeth and use the powder to start a fire. But I knew starting a fire would be difficult as we were on a low hammock, and everything was wet. It was still raining, and we prepared for a long night. Then I heard the wonderful sound of an ax hitting a dry buttonwood log, not over a half a mile away. "Likker still, hot diggedy dog! Let's go!" We put a sack on our boat pole and stuck it up so we could find the boat again and started walking toward where the ax choppin' was coming from. We walked though mangroves, ponds, buttonwoods, and sawgrass without a light, stumbling around a lot. Before long we could see the glow of a liquor still fire across a ten-acre pond. We let them know by hollering who we were, and they sent a whiskey scow after us. We knew them, otherwise they wouldn't have come for us; they had plenty of grits and pork chops. We dried out and took two or three sips of their 'shine and spent the night. That ax chopping was a lovely sound. But, I would never have chopped a dry log if that had been me, would'a been afraid the wrong people would hear it. I took as few chances as possible.

*   *   *

During those days in the 1920s and '30s, you had to be closemouthed about moonshiners and everything else. Anyway, what they did was their business and none of mine. Although I came across many of these men in my travels, I knew to keep my mouth shut. If I'd been married, I wouldn't have told my wife about them.[6] From 1916, when they put the first part of the Ingraham Highway in, until 1933, there were lots of whiskey stills in the Bill Ashley Jungles—at different times. This was a favorite spot for moonshiners since they could put their scows in along the road and travel back into the mangroves and glades undetected. Whiskey making off the Ingraham Highway started as early as Prohibition, or before. And that riverhead country suited the situation [in the Bill Ashley Jungles]. Scows, sixteen feet long, four feet wide, and about a foot deep, could carry stills, sugar, and corn. I've been told that a lot depended on timing: meeting the supply truck, unloading, loading, and moving on. If they ever left their vehicles on the road, I never seen it. How many stills were there at one time is hard to say. But if I was walking along the road, fishing for bass in the late 1920s, I could hear the sound of a pitcher pump pumping water in the condenser barrel. Some of the pumps could be noisy if you worked them too hard. I can't write the sound, but if you ever heard a pitcher pump, you know the sound. Kinda like *uunk-uunk*. Some stills were within a couple hundred yards from the road straight out, but the trails could be winding and long—some maybe a half mile. These jungles weren't the only still sites by far. Much spirits were made closer to town. Moonshiners moved often, for the most part. This rockland country [pinewoods closer to Homestead] was spotted with old dried-up gator holes and hammocks, and most every one of them, at one time or more, had had stills in them. I saw many old still sites before the pinelands were cleared. A lot of spirits was being made long after the repeal of Prohibition. After Prohibition was repealed in 1933, the few stills that were busy were moved often to confuse the prohis.

Some moonshiners used six-barrel pots, which were preferably made of copper. The prohis tore these pots up so often that many moonshiners used cheaper pots made from galvanized tin. Of course this galvanized tin was poison, so 'twas said, but the moonshiners didn't care about this. They even started using car radiators instead of coils. From the stills I visited, most used up to about forty barrels of mash. The word was if everything was done right, a barrel of mash or "buck" would turn out six gallons of sellable 'shine—more if you cut it weak. After Prohibition was repealed and legal spirits were available, most moonshiners dropped out, but some kept on. Old habits die hard.

The prohis were trouble to me as I was stopped and searched often. By being closemouthed about what I did and knew, I got by. But the prohis would stop me now and then and go through my stuff—whether I was in a glade skiff or vehicle. They would even visit my camps with game wardens. They were really hot to catch me since I looked guilty because I stayed in the swamps so much. Making moonshine was a rough business. So they were really hot to catch the moonshiners. I remember hearing about a shoot-out on the Ingraham Highway, near the Bill Ashley Jungles, where three men were killed. These killings took place about 1925. One lad, a neighbor of ours named Clyde Parrish, was about nineteen years old—and that's as old as he got. Parrish came driving up the road near the Jennings Farm east of the Bill Ashley Jungles. He was stopped by the prohis. It was going around that Clyde tried to swim the canal to get behind a rock bank but was shot in the water. There was three men killed that time by the prohis. His mother and sisters tried to get in touch with him through a medium of spirits. One of those table knockers. There was a lot of hocus-pocus in those days, besides the hellishness.

But I never made 'shine. I loved my freedom more than money. A year and a day in an Atlanta prison wasn't for me, and that was the penalty for being caught. People were so hellish in them days, some of my acquaintances probably would have planted some 'shine in my Model A Ford if they hadn't liked 'shine so well themselves.

During the Depression, people were panhandling on the streets of Homestead, and you learned early who to watch out for. If not, it could cost you. These fellows had developed a taste for alcohol, cigarettes, easy living, and lying. They'd try to convince you that they'd found a lake full of gators and only needed a couple of dollars for "bread and bullets." Well, to shorten this up, they never paid you back. They would try to flag me down if I was driving down the main street—but I knew to keep going. They learned what you were doing, and you knew what they weren't doing.

Along about then, I cooked out some gator grease and filled a beer bottle with some of it. This was some foul-smelling stuff that I hoped to give to a beerhead that I knew who owed me money. This fella used to always sit in front of the Last Chance Saloon, and I was going to put it in front of him. Even if he didn't take a sip of it, the smell would kill him. I hauled it around for months in the floorboards of my Model A Ford.

Well, I never used it for what it was intended—but it did come in handy after one gator-hunting trip that I went on with Buck Rohrer. We were camped in the headwaters of the East River in the Bill Ashley Jungles near Nobles Still.[7] I think we got about fifty flat skins that trip and a bunch of shorts, about a hundred hides in all. This ain't much for two weeks, but it seemed a lot at the time. After we had been walk-hunting for two weeks, we went back to the road by glade skiff. It was so shallow on that trip, we mostly walked and pulled the boat. At the road, we loaded up the Model A and cranked its engine. We had gone about a mile or so, and whether Buck noticed it or not—and I think he did, there was a black stream of oil behind the Model A on the white, rock road. We hadn't gone over a mile, our oil was gone and we stopped just in time. Someone had loosened the oil plug hoping we'd burn out the bearings, and it's a sure wonder it didn't happen. Buck walked back and found the oil plug, and that's when the gator grease came in handy. We mixed some canal water with the gator grease and ran the Model A on it. It was able to carry us the twenty-five miles home, running slow. Later, I put some kerosene in the oil pan and ran it for a few minutes but it continued to stink like gator grease. There was some hellish people in them days.

When in the woods, you always had to worry about what condition your car would be in when you returned. Now that old Ingraham Highway wasn't traveled much—maybe a dozen cars a week and most of them were on the weekends. Most times, we parked the car down in the mangroves, about twenty-five miles from Homestead. Once after a few-week glade skiff trip, Buck and I came back to the road, and the hood was up on the Model A. "Now what the hell?" There, sitting on the motor, was a brand new fan belt. Somebody had needed a fan belt, taken ours, and then bought us a new one—but had neglected to put it on. We pretty much figured out who that was, and later he owned up to it and had a good excuse. This fella had a Model A ton truck, a fish truck, which he used since he fished out of Flamingo. I met him at the Last Chance Saloon and casually asked, "Why didn't you put that fan belt back on?" He talked with a lisp and replied, "The skeeters just 'bout eat me up that night, I just laid it on top and got out of there."

When on these two-week trips, often some common man would siphon off your gasoline when you left your rattle-trap vehicle on the road to fend for itself. I learned early to hide enough gasoline in the bushes to get home. 'Twas said that a gator hunter's service station was a siphon hose and a five-gallon can.

*   *   *

Only one trail that early prowlers used has been reopened—the Hell's Bay Trail. It was on the trip I took with Buck Rohrer into the Nobles Still area that we discovered this trail that led from West Lake into Pearl Bay through the headwaters of the East River. The riverhead had some prongs that at one time led into West Lake. The Ingraham Highway had cut the riverheads in two in several places. At night, Buck and I talked about how a man with a small narrow boat could have crossed the state from Garfield Bight to Whitewater Bay—if he had little else to do and was damn fool enough. I had traveled in that country, on the trails that led to Pearl Bay, with other men—Lige Powers and Ed

Gladesmen at a surveyors' camp in Big Cypress, 1924. Argyle Hendry (second from left), Bill Ashley (fourth from left), Ran Henderson (with banjo), Oren Brady (holding gun), D. M. Henderson (second from right).

Brooker. We had never seen a map of the East River or heard the name "Hell's Bay Trail." But we always had a job getting through from the road to the main river. This trail twisted and turned worser than any snake and was grown thick with mangroves.

The government cut that trail out in the 1960s, after I told Dr. Craighead about it. It was later written that he had discovered this trail from West Lake to Pearl Bay. I don't know who the first men through this route were—as we never found any cut marks or sign of man at all. When guiding Dr. Craighead in this area, I told him of my discussion with Buck but not of the gator hunting. It shouldn't be forgotten that men like to explore, and some men went to any length to find out what lay ahead. Now the old-timers are all dead, or almost.

Gladesmen

When I was fourteen or fifteen years old, I mostly threw in with older men that were at home in the swamps. I took up with a few fellows that had turned into misfits for the love of moonshine. Others that I traveled with never or seldom took a drink. For the most part, I enjoyed the companionship of all of them. Homestead was well represented with ragged and patched clothes—wearing men. Some were bad off, others were better fixed but wore old clothes to fit in with their neighbors and discourage panhandlers. These men seemed to come into town early, get the news of the day, and then scatter out to the fishing holes, little pothole gardens, and the swamps. They must have had a little old pension from World War I or something. Most managed to get tobacco—which came before eating in them days. Men would rather tighten their belts than give up smoking. A man with some tailor-made smokes had plenty of friends. Even so, with a sack of Bull Durham, it was better to stay out of town. In those days there were many men who lived like that—outside of town, in a little old shack or something. Although some had places near town, they were really at home in the swamps. But you can't live like that anymore.

I used to ramble around a little with a man named Lige Powers. Lige was probably in his forties when I started going out in the swamp with him. I hunted and camped with him from 1934 until about 1937. Lige was small, wiry, and dark. If he ever owned more than what was on his back, I never knew it. I'm not throwing off on him, that's just the way it was. Lige didn't even have a gun. If he was hunting, he'd go with someone and borrow their gun. When he bought a pair of pants, he'd take off the ones he had on and throw them away. The only time I ever saw him take a bath was when a gator turned us over.

The Reef Country, about half mile or so north of Florida Bay, is kind of poor country for growth and game. The buttonwood snags in

West Lake hunting camp, late 1930s. Courtesy Alexander Sprunt IV.

there are so sharp and hard, they'd skin a coon. After Lige tore his seat and the seat of his britches on one of these snags, he said, "Now, maybe the gnats will stay out of my face." We made it to a sports-fishing camp that was on Mud Creek about a mile northeast of Little Madeira Bay. There, on a nail, hung a dirty pair of pants, and Lige did a swap job. He never seemed to want but what he had on. I wonder what that feller said when he found them tore up britches. I write about Lige only because he's long since dead, and he can't debunk these stories. He never talked about his past to me, but he sure had one—he was well scarred. His back was badly burned. No doubt he'd had his troubles. A few years later Lige Powers was drowned while gill net fishing.

We stayed lost a lot in the mangroves and rivers and Lige said, "Good! Now maybe we'd find sompin." And sometimes we did. When you're feeling out them mangroves, and there's no set way to go, you can go a long way—and get a short distance. Before the 1935 storm [the Labor Day Hurricane], we would always climb a tree and get our bearings by spotting the palms on Seven Palm Lake—that is if we were within five miles. There was a couple of palms left there after the storm. Most everywhere in the open glades there were landmarks to guide you, but there were few in the mangroves. Although sometimes in the winter we could hear the shotguns of the duck hunters at their West Lake camp. The duck camp was there from 1916 through the 1930s. In the early morning, we could hear their shots for ten miles—when the air drift was right.

Lige Powers was a master at gathering food. He could tell by the bubbles in the water just what was on the bottom. He'd simply lean over the side of the boat, grab a turtle, and bring it into the boat. He liked sliders best; of course they had many names: chicken turtles, hard shell cooters, streaked necks. These were good fried, but when we were short on grease we stewed them with rice. We had to live cheaply and having enough lard for a two- or three-week trip was a problem. A three-pound bucket of Jewel lard didn't go too far when making bread and frying meat.

Lige had a way of easing a mean situation. Everything seemed to go against us on some of our long trips poling through the mangroves in a glade boat. The skeeters would be bad; it would be hot, rainy; the smudge bucket was always contrary; and the drinking water rotten. There are many blind cuts in the mangroves and sometimes after cutting, pulling, and poling for over an hour, the run would peter out, and you knew you had to dead-head back out. Nothing to do but growl and get with it. Lige might laugh and ask, "How about a little smile?" It helped.

Once Lige's joking around got me in trouble. We were glade skiffing throughout the mangrove and buttonwood country northeast of Cuthbert Lake in 1935. We had been traveling all through the Bill Ashley Jungles along the Reef—killing a few gators and otter. The glade skiff takes a lot of maneuvering in that country, as very little straight waterways can be found. When Lige was poling, he would talk to the boat as if it was alive, and he had named the boat after a friend's wife. Said friend owned the boat and kept it hid along the Ingraham Highway, about a half mile south of Ed Brooker's Landing. The boat was in a handy place, so we used it for a few trips. The name given to the boat must be changed here to protect the innocent and me. This lady had an elongated behind, and Lige had no doubt noticed it. He would oftentimes say to the boat, "All right Carrie, get your long butt around here," when he was working the boat through the crooks and turns. Well damn fool me, I picked this habit up. Throughout these trips I used it—and it was all right, broke the monotony. Well, it was all right till sometime later when I was on a trip with the lady's husband, and umm ba ha . . . wouldn't you know it, out popped "Get your long butt around here, Carrie." No sooner was that said that I wished I was dead and thought I would soon be. His head turned around like a whip snapping. I gazed off into the swamp knowing I'd played hell. Finally, he turned back toward the bow, and I breathed again. I never thought about anything else the rest of the trip. He never brought it up, and I sure didn't. Sixty years have passed but these mistakes are never forgotten.

* * *

Lige and I never spent much more than five or six dollars on a two- or three-week trip. That included twelve cans of Prince Albert Tobacco, one hundred pounds of salt (for salting down the gator hides), and two boxes of .22 bullets. Salt was seventy-five cents for a hundred pounds at Red's dry cleaning shop. Prince Albert tobacco went for a dollar for twelve cans at the A & P store. We paid twenty-five to thirty-five cents a box for .22 bullets. And bacon squares or smoked hog jowls were a few cents a pound.

Lige always did the shooting, he didn't miss! We used a few of our shotgun shells for meat and otters in the winter. We'd get some "hog taters," little sweet potatoes that were too small for market. Bananas grew wild around mule pens in the farmlands that dotted the glades during the '30s. Sometimes we'd bring a sack of oranges or grapefruit. A friend of ours at Flamingo sometimes would let us have a few smoked mullet and a few pieces of salted sea cow [manatee].

On one trip in November of 1934, Lige and I started out at Whiskey Creek (this is the park name, but it was the main jumping-off place in the Bill Ashley Jungles). We went on this trip to hunt otters. Lige wanted to stay in as close to Cuthbert Lake and Seven Palm Lake as we could get. We left the Reef Trail and went further in toward the lakes. There was few trails in there and there was no way to tell except by guessing. He was hoping we'd find more gators and otters along there, as most glade-skiff traveling was done along the Reef. And since the Reef was the main trail, there wasn't much stuff there. At least three boats a year went through there. But on that trip we'd really had it. The water was really low since the rains had shut down early. The water is different every year in that country. One year, a camper might get some good water to drink at the mouth of Taylor Creek. But at the same time the next year, the water would be brine salty.

When we pulled into the upper part of Taylor Creek, about a half day's pole from Little Madeira Bay, the water was slightly brackish. We knew that we weren't going to find any better water that day in this creek. We filled a gallon paint bucket anyway and went on. Later that day, and about two miles from the creek's mouth, the water was salty, and our bucket was dry. We spent the night at Argyle Hendry's old camp on Taylor Creek needing drinking water.

We left at daylight without eating. The air plants give us a little bad water and chewing on onion orchards helped. The weather was holding hot, and I willingly would have traded it all for a gallon of water. Lige's good humor held, and he continued to poke around for some water. We didn't hunt anything, just kept looking for water. By following the Eastern Creek Route [also called the Interior Route], instead of going around in the bay, Lige hoped to find water fit to drink.

When we got as far north as could be without useless work, Lige carried a paint bucket in hand and said, "Shoot me up, if I ain't back by sundown." By shooting into the air, he'd know where I was. Then he headed north on foot. After I fought skeeters and chewed on orchard bulbs for three or four hours, Lige returned with not a drop of water in the bucket.

We left and poled steady for about three or four miles through Joe Bay, Snag Bay, and then north into the Wink Eye Creek. To get into the Wink Eye Creek, we had to lay down in the boat and pull ourselves under the mangroves. We finally reached the Wink Eye Creek by sundown and got some drinking water. Lige said, "Thank you, Lord." He thanked the Lord often. We killed a few gators in the Wink Eye and left after a few days.

We took the shortcut into Long Sound from the Wink Eye Creek. After a day's pole we ended up at Jewfish Creek, where we headed toward Argyle Hendry's camp on Lake Surprise.[8] The reason we were going to Hendry's camp was because Lige wanted to take a deer ham to old Argyle. Lige nursemaided the ham for eight or nine days. He'd smoke it at night, and then he'd cover it up with cabbage palms and wax myrtle during the day. That's how he'd keep it from spoiling.

Hendry caught a crocodile now and then and also rented boats to people. But he didn't rent many boats since he didn't have any good ones. When we neared his place, the old man seen us coming down the canal. People called Argyle "Mr. Hendry" to his face, but they called him "Hogeye" behind his back—his eyes were very small and squinty.

Anyway we stopped. Lige was anxious to give him that ham. We

Argyle Hendry at his sister's house in Cutler, Florida, early 1940s.

got out on the railroad bed. Hendry was on the other side of the railroad bed with his houseboat. We walked across the railroad bed. Lige had that ham in his hand. He yelled from the door of his houseboat for us to come in. He spoke with such a nasal twang you could hardly understand him. He was glad to see somebody. We brought the deer ham and got inside that houseboat, and boy did it stink. Umm, umm, it did stink. We went right on back outside.

I said, "Mr. Hendry what in the world is that smell in there?" He said, "Why I don't know. Oh yes, the skeeters were too bad last night, so instead of going outside to do my business I just messed in my smudge pot." That's just what he said. But that's the way people lived in those days. I don't guess he could smell too good—he had a bad adenoids or something.

*   *   *

Lige and Argyle often rambled around together. On one occasion, when hunting in the mangroves, Lige Powers and Hogeye Hendry had to decide if a cave was occupied by an alligator or a crocodile. These men were two of the best woodsmen there ever was. Although they weren't agreeing, Hendry had the last word—him being the oldest and most experienced in the art of making the most out of what the country had to offer. The two men had made their way through the Wink Eye Creek to where it widens out some half mile or so north of Snag Bay. This part of the Wink Eye Creek is a marginal area between the salt and freshwater, and this is why they didn't know which animal was in the cave. The water in the cave was shaking and muddy, which let them know it was occupied. They began a whispering conversation; Mr. Hendry, talking through his nose, said, "Crocodile." Lige said, "Alligator." After the heated "ya-ya," Mr. Hendry had his way.

If it was a crocodile, they'd catch him—as they were worth more alive. Now catching a live crocodile requires penning off the cave from behind the mouth with iron bars and then digging a hole about a foot in diameter behind those bars. After digging the hole, you have to use a slender rod to prod the croc toward the hole. Usually, the croc was then grabbed at the hole with a hook and tied up. It takes a lot of work. On the other hand, if it was a gator they'd a-run him out of the cave with a rod and shoot him.

After considerable work in the heat and the skeeters, they were ready to hook that crocodile. Lige began feeling for the reptile with the rod. He motioned to Hendry, letting him know that he'd stuck something, and it was coming toward the hole. Hendry then felt with his hook and raised it. Through his nose he said, "I got him Lige." Then Lige heard him growl, "God blame soft-shell turtle."

* * *

Hendry had a number of camps around, and he wasn't the cleanest camper in the world. In the fall of 1944, my wife and I towed two glade boats behind a little launch with a small Briggs motor up the Taylor Creek behind Little Madeira Bay. We also had a bitch with seven puppies and a house cat with us. You could hardly skin a gator in camp because the seven puppies were all over it eating and fighting. We were planning to stay at Argyle Hendry's old campsite on Fresh Water Creek for three weeks—hunting gator and otter and just plain living. The water there is fresh, at least when the water was up in the glades—and it was up on this trip.

When the buzzards flew up as we neared the campsite, we knew somebody had been there recently. It didn't take long to figure out that it had to have been Mr. Argyle Hendry. We soon noticed that there were two lines tied to some bushes that were running off into the creek. When we pulled the lines in, one had a pair of long handle drawers on it—that's the way Mr. Hendry washed his clothes. And damned if a hard-shell cooter, with a hole bored through its shell, wasn't tied to the other. I cut the cooter loose and threw the drawers away.

Mr. Hendry must have been gone from this camp for about a month or so. The buzzards had stomped the bushes down, maybe to have a clean place to mess. Needless to say, the camp was a mess and not just from the many tobacco chews. But we were able to clean the place up and enjoy it. Sometime after that I asked Mr. Hendry why in the devil he did such a thing as tying up that poor old turtle and leaving him to starve. His answer, "You never know when you might come back there and need something to eat. But the drawers, just plum forgot them. Did you bring them with you?" That reminded me of something Eugene Saunders told me about Mr. Hendry. Seems that Mr. Hendry was camped on Manatee Creek near Eugene Saunders's fish camp. Saunders saw him standing there with a ham under his arm, cutting out some maggots. When he was asked about it, he replied, "Just a little live-stock in there."

Another one of my hunting partners was Buck Rohrer; he was closer to my age, and we often found trouble. Seems like every time Buck Rohrer and I went into Little Madeira Bay, things didn't turn out good. On one trip, in August of 1935, we just didn't use our good judgment. We were staying at the bottom of the bay in the cabbage woods [cabbage palms]. Now, let me say, this ain't a delightful time of year to camp and fire-hunt that country. It was hot, rainy, and buggy, and we had no tarpaulin. The skeeters are so thick, one fellow said, if you wanted to talk to the other fellow, you could throw a coconut and talk through the hole it made through the air.

But Buck was good about jumping out of the skeeter bar at daylight and getting a fire and smoke going. Then I'd get up and tend to the kitchen chores. We would also skin what few gators we had in the morning. On one morning, Buck jumped out and really started feeding those skeeters. He then grabbed a few dry cabbage fronds, set 'em on fire, and said, "I'll show you how to kill some skeeters." He started waving the fired fronds around, trying to burn up those skeeters. I was still in the skeeter bar, enjoying the show when Buck played hell. He waved the fronds too close to the bar, and the bar caught fire. Since it was already sagging with the weight of a jillion skeeters, the skeeter bar was lying close to me. With a "whoosh," that bar was slap burnt off me in a second.

With no skeeter bar, we knew it was time to make tracks out of there. With all the mistakes we made sometimes I wonder how we made a living way back then. Seems like we lived on "belch and little else." Somebody said they lived on love and leftovers, but we had neither of these, at least me.

On another trip with Buck, we brought his wife and baby girl along. We poled two glade skiffs to the Camp Bill Ashley on the Joe River for a two-week gator hunt and carried what water we could in the small boats and our little still. Most times you wouldn't need a still—only in the dry springtime. But we were staying for a few weeks and figured the water that was available might be brackish. During this trip, Buck's wife, Ruth, would run the still twice a day while we were in the swamp

A glade skiff along side the Ingraham Highway at Taylor Slough, outside of Palm Hammock (now Royal Palm Hammock in Everglades National Park), early 1900s. Courtesy Arva Moore Parks.

Audubon warden heading up Taylor Creek, late 1930s. Courtesy Alexander Sprunt IV.

hunting and run off a few gallons of water. You could rig up a still from a five-gallon can, a coil of three-eighths copper tubing, and a lard-can suitcase. A little flour paste helped to keep it from leaking steam. Well now, I could get used to this, a cook in the camp and a still operator too. But once the smoke from the still firing was seen, and then Ruth had the company of a bunch of deer hunters. This was the only time we was found, but nothing come of it. A few days later, according to her, she was filling the still with river water, and it pulled out of her hands. When she got it off the bottom of the river, it was all bent in like it had been beat with a stick. She had it by the handle, and it was sucked out of her hand. What the hell happened, I don't know. We pried it out a little with sticks run through the lid hole, and she run it a few more times, making a lot less water. Sure was spooky. It must have created a vacuum from the hot steam. That was the only time Buck took his wife with us. I've seen whiskey stills after the prohis got through with them that didn't look much worse. That can was a five-gallon galvanized and pretty tough—but it had made its last trip.

Camping in the Taylor Slough

Most of the water from Taylor Slough ends up in the Little Madeira Bay. The water doesn't travel very fast in the slough because of the thick wall of mangroves around it. Taylor Creek, a little old creek, doesn't get much water coming into it like it used to—the heavy growth mangroves slows it. I used to fish in that creek a little bit. It's an oddball place, so overhung with mangroves. The thickness there is good 'cause it keeps all the water from getting out of the Everglades.

Taylor Slough is the name used now, but everyone hereabouts used the name "Dead Pecker Slough" instead. Even the women used this name. I guess they heard it from the men folks and didn't know what they were talking about. Ed Brooker was the one who told me about how the slough got that name. Ed Brooker was always right in the thick of things; he was wild as the devil as a young man. Well, back in the teens through the '20s, there was a big tomato-farming operation west of Palm Hammock called the Blue Goose Farm [in the Hole-in-the-Donut, a former agricultural area in Everglades National Park]. They had a rooming house there for the help, a packinghouse, and they laid wooden railroad tracks through the soft glade from the packinghouse to the fields. They didn't use a train but used mules to haul the tomatoes on a cart along those tracks. The cart had train wheels. Well, there were always a few ladies in business there—prostitutes hanging out at the Blue Goose. Because of this situation, somebody came

Aerial photograph of the Madeira Farms on the south side of the Ingraham Highway, 1940. The highway turns due west at this point, after heading southwest from Palm Hammock. Courtesy Everglades National Park.

up with that expression—"dead pecker slough"—when they were driving across it one day. The name stuck, or so Ed Brooker told me.

After the road to Flamingo had been finished a few years, some local people decided to drain and farm part of the Taylor Slough. The part of the slough they tried to drain was about three miles southwest of the Palm Hammock.[9] Five to seven miles of ditches were put in with large ditching equipment and one large pump. They only dug the ditches to the rock where it was deep, which was about six or seven feet deep through solid mud and in some places peat. But where the marl was shallow, they dug down several feet into the rock. The farm workers were to live in three small, one-room shacks. These shacks were built on stilts a quarter of a mile east of where the road to Flamingo turned due west. The road to the farm hands' quarters was the only road built. It wasn't much. Before anything was planted the whole operation was called off. It didn't take long to find out that there was better doings somewhere else. The boom had busted. As one man said, "The bloom was off the rose."

We all called the part of the Taylor Slough where the ditches were dug the "Madeira Farms" since the water from the slough ran down to Little Madeira Bay. As I said, this very wet property of the Madeira Farms was never actually farmed. It's doubtful if even one collard plant was ever planted there. But what this network of ditches raised was wildlife, it turned into a wildlife bonanza [because fish and game were attracted to the ditches' deeper water, particularly during the dry season]. Everything flourished here for many years. The fish alone could have fed thousands of people. The slough was a rich place for deer, gators, otter, coons, native ducks, limpkins, and night herons by the thousands. There were large flocks of curlews [white ibis], short whites [snowy egrets], flint heads or gannets [wood storks], long whites [great egrets], po joes [great blue herons],[10] water turkeys [anhingas], and many bitterns.

But with the boom-time ditches that were closer to town, only a few people used this area to fish. I often hunted in the Madeira Farms, and we always put our boats in at the Madeira Farms jumping-off place where the Ingraham Highway made a sharp westward turn at the el-

A camp at the northeastern corner of the Madeira Farms, 1934. This road-ditch headed a quarter mile due east from the Ingraham Highway.

bow of Taylor Slough, or at Palm Hammock. There was a small hammock there then, it's gone now, where we could hide our boats. After seventy years, the ditches are overgrown and filled in by leaves and silt. A man would have a hard time making a living there now—since there's little wildlife left.

This was a kind of mean country, and very few people used this area for hunting. A man had to bog a lot or push a glade skiff when the water was up. And sometimes the water was high year-round. Gator fleas were also really bad in Taylor Slough. Even though a gator flea is just a little fellow, one-fourth the size of your little fingernail, when he does his thing you would sit down in a nest of cotton mouths to get your shoe off and get rid of him. A red-hot fire coal would seem like a piece of ice compared to a gator flea between your toes. And I've had many of them. Oh! If I could have only had a camcorder on some of them fellows—and me too.

I learned early that the best way to bog the glades was barefooted as the fleas could be got rid of in a hurry. They seem to prefer people wearing loose top boots. However, barefooted ain't too good where there are crawdads. When they start pinching your feet it's hard to stay still, which you have to or else you'll scare a gator that's coming to the top. A gator can feel every movement in that spongy country. Your worst enemy when barefooted was sawgrass. A sawgrass cut was slow to heal and sore.

Ted Walker and I, in the spring of 1934 or '35, had made our way to the Madeira Farms jumping-off place. We had enough grub to last a few days. We were eating a bite before setting out on a few days' walk when a Seminole named Charlie Billie came along. It was common in those days for white hide buyers from Miami to drop Indian gator hunters off at the Madeira Farms and other places and then pick them up in a few days to buy their hides. Billie had been waiting there all day, and the hide buyer hadn't picked him up. [11] They had been on a four-day gator hunt. He said, "Four sleeps, four gators," so we knew that he hadn't had much luck. Billie had a broken wrist that had never been set. It hung limp and was useless. We offered him something to eat. We had told him to help his self, and he did. He gathered up both of our sacks and started walking toward the hammock. Ted and I done nothing but look at one another then we took off after him. When we got to the hammock, we saw one other man and two yearling boys, about nine and ten years, in a nearby camp. We watched them eat our food, and then we left. [12]

We only stayed in Madeira Farms for two days on that trip. It was a hardship trip, and we had to eat some staples I had buried at a camp further on in the slough. Some years later I saw in the paper that an Indian's bones were found in a dugout canoe north of the Tamiami Trail in Willow Slough. I knew it was Billie since the article said that his wrist was broken. I met Billie on several occasions in the glades. He seemed to like the Taylor Slough, although the Indians never camped there for long periods since it was such a mean country. Just a few days and they were gone. They would go long distances on foot in a few days on short rations. However, I've found a few small sites of ancient Indians in that country.

Glen at his Madeira Farms camp, 1935. This structure was made from fertilizer sacks soaked in cement; it could be taken apart and moved.

*　　*　　*

A few years later, in 1938, I got back to the road from hunting in the Taylor Slough when I found five FBI men waiting for me—with guns. I was easing up to the road that day, poling a twenty-six-foot Seminole dugout canoe. The canoe had some gator hides as they were still legal. But I had hidden a deer about a quarter mile back from the road as they were out of season. I was fifteen miles from town and hoped to get a ride. I was pretty sure I'd have to walk the three miles to Palm Hammock and then catch a ride back to town with one of the men farming there—if I was lucky. Later, I'd have to get someone to come back with me to get that deer.

When the canoe hit the bank, the FBI men jumped up and surrounded me. Because of the deer, my heart beat double time. I'd been gone a week or so and didn't know about the Cash kidnapping, and they didn't tell me anything except that they were FBI. [13] They asked me how long I'd been gone and if I'd seen anyone on the trip. Course I hadn't. I was uneasy, as it seemed like somebody was always trying to get me for something. I figured they were prohis except they wore plain clothes. A little moonshining was still going on, and the government was all out to stop it.

These FBI men just shook their heads when I asked them for a ride. Maybe I smelled too bad. So, I walked up to Palm Hammock and luckily met a truck at the Big Bend Road. A farmer who was planting sweet potatoes told me about the Cash baby, Skeegie, being kidnapped and gave me a ride. He said the woods were swarming with FBI men. His explanation cleared things up about what happened at the landing.

Somebody must have told the FBI where I'd be landing as it was pretty well hid from the road. Seemed like every trip was trouble. When you're living outdoors, somebody's always meddling with you and would try to put the law on you. But as I've said before, many hellish people were in this neck of the woods, and they seemed to live just to cause trouble. Being a coward and sneaky and by ramblin' alone kept me out of trouble a lot of times.

Cuthbert Lake Area

We came into these lakes mostly from fall through April.[14] Pole-hunting was done by walking mostly in the spring but some was done all year in a marsh that suited the situation.[15] In the winter if the water was up and the price of otter or gator hides was worthwhile, we could jump off from a few different landings using glade skiffs. We'd wind up many miles and weeks later at another landing. Sometimes we'd land where the railroad met the highway on Key Largo—where someone might meet us or a ride could be caught. Other times we'd land at the Ingraham Highway around the East River headwaters. A good landing and jumping-off place was the old Madeira Farms, and it was used often. From there we could get to Seven Palm Lake and Little Madeira Bay, and if you was wanting to real bad you could beat your way into Cuthbert and land at the West Lake landing. We could only use these routes when we had enough water to pole or drag the boats.

Wood storks at Cuthbert Lake Rookery, late 1930s. Courtesy Alexander Sprunt IV.

The trips didn't always pay off, as on one hard, cold trip into the Cuthbert Lake country in December of 1936. Lige Powers and myself left the road at the West Lake landing. We were poling a twenty-six-foot dugout canoe that I owned and had bought for ten dollars on credit. This dugout canoe was paid for years later with interest. There was a commercial duck camp at the West Lake landing. West Lake might be about three miles long. A creek ties West Lake to East Lake; another creek midways along East Lake ties it to Cuthbert Lake.[16] On this trip, the wind was blowing from the northwest for so long that the water was shaking so bad we couldn't fire-hunt.

We camped on an old campground on the east bank of Cuthbert where the creek from East Lake enters it. The Audubon people had stayed here during the nesting season, but they were now gone—as were the birds from the rookery. They had nailed "keep out" signs aplenty, though. Most outlying people were always wary of game wardens of any kind. The Audubon warden was there to keep anyone

Raccoons at a camp along the Ingraham Highway, winter 1934. The camp was located in a small cypress stand, west of the Madeira Farms.

away from the rookery—although there was no market for feathers or plumes at that date. Gators hung around the rookery, and I suppose the warden didn't want any shooting around there as it would disturb the birds. This rookery was active even after the 1935 storm. Many egrets, cranes [larger egrets and herons], and curlews nested here. On this trip there was just a few cormorants with babies. All the other birds had left after nesting.

Shotgun shells were scarce in the camp on that trip. We asked several duck hunters if they could spare a few shells. We got a handful. Most of the duck hunters were in West Lake. We mostly talked to the ones that came by the camp. They didn't like to be disturbed if sitting in a blind. Lige wanted to save the few shells we had to shoot otters with.

We were hunting anything that we thought we could sell. We even got a few coons. At that time, they were almost worthless. I shipped some to Sears Roebuck and the F. C. Taylor Fur Company and received from five cents to twenty-five cents apiece. That was the last coons for me. Otters returned from five to seven dollars each. The Depression was on.

Since shells was scarce, we decided to get some baby cormorants to eat by pushing them out of the nests with a boat pole. Lige pushed the dugout stern first under the mangroves of the rookery. (We used the dugout in the lakes and waterways where the turns were not too sharp.) But what Lige wanted to do didn't work—as the birds wouldn't fall through. Then Lige decided to use a shotgun and burn up a shell by firing across a nest. When he had things lined up right he let her go. He then climbed into the mangroves and returned to the boat with two squabs. Lige had on a black suit coat—as most crackers wore them in them days—but it wasn't black anymore. He was whitewashed with bird manure—his black beard and hat, everything was white. When I asked him if he wanted to jump overboard and clean up, he just pointed

West Lake Landing, late 1930s. Courtesy Alexander Sprunt IV.

toward the camp. That was the first and last I ever ate. Some things in life, once is enough. Even the very young are fishy tasting.

*   *   *

On this trip we worked our way from the West Lake landing through East Lake, Cuthbert, down into The Lungs (a lake), and then over to Garfield Bight. We fire-hunted all these lakes and creeks—but didn't have much luck. I got to thinking as to why we didn't find much gators in these lakes: West, East, Cuthbert, and The Lungs. After the cotton pickers put the road in, the motorboat boys could reach Alligator Creek real easy.[17] Near the mouth was some gator bones, probably a month old, where the motorboat boys had skinned out a few. We found the bones by the buzzards. This happened often since it was so easy to get to Alligator Creek by the cotton road and launch a boat. And it didn't make for good thinking to work out these waterways by pole boats. I don't imagine the motorboat boys always done good either as these waterways were worked too hard, too often. We made very little money on this trip as it had been gator hunted not long before. Someone had done better than us. Later during the war, with the rationing that went on in the meat markets, fish were in demand and brought much better prices. Fish wasn't rationed so the backwoods boys were laying off the gators, at least somewhat, and I had a better crack at these waterways up until the park came in 1947.

*   *   *

Later in the spring, I traveled with Buck Rohrer back into the Cuthbert Lake country. We had talked about this trip in town—thinking we could make a good payday there. Buck was always rarin' to go. We'd get to the camp, it would be only two hours before nightfall, and he'd say, "I'm going to get a gator before dark." And he would, while I cleaned out the campground. And we did do all right on this trip—the hell-westers hadn't been there yet.[18] Most men won't go where they can't take motors. They like to stay in the saddle like cowboys. They don't want to do nothing off their horsepower.

It was a low water spring. Buck and me poled one glade skiff six miles to Liquor Still Creek on the northeast corner of Cuthbert Lake.

The water in Cuthbert might be a little brackish, but most times good drinking water could be had in the creek. Now the creek got its name from a huge liquor still made from a large steel tank of around a thousand gallons. It was so tough the prohis couldn't do much damage with axes, so it was shot full of holes. These holes were plugged up, and the still was run some more. For many years that old pot could be seen half buried in the mud of the lake.

We traveled about a half mile up to where Liquor Still Creek's headwaters broke out of the heavy buttonwood and mangroves into a good gator marsh (we called it Cuthbert Marsh). We usually reached this marsh from the north, jumping off from the Madeira Farms or the Bill Ashley Jungles. Since we hadn't walked into the lake area, we didn't know how chock-a-block that creek was with buttonwood logs. It took a half a day to get to the open glades through this creek. We pulled and lifted the boat over the fallen logs and found few places where we could boat. This creek was about six or seven feet wide and not over a half a mile long. I doubt if this creek is active anymore. And it may be lost or gone forever. Maybe it just grew shut.

After hitting the glade, we camped on a dry clump at the end of Liquor Still Creek. We walked for two weeks, mostly going northwest to northeast and between Cuthbert and Seven Palm as far easterly as the little freshwater lake that lies a quarter mile north of Seven Palm Lake—never being over three miles from camp. We never had a name for this little lake of about ten acres, it was just called Little Freshwater Lake. Our camp was about a mile from the head of the creek that flows into Seven Palm Lake. That way we could hunt the two creeks and the glades. We always split up the marsh and walked alone. We found no recognizable sign of any hunting or man sign on the trip; but knowing man's nature, I'm sure man had been here. We did well on this trip but never again come into Cuthbert Marsh from Cuthbert Lake; although we did come here from the north, when the water was up, by glade skiff. If Ed Brooker hadn't took me through this marsh from a trail through the Reef, I would never have known about it.

On the way back to the lake, tired and sweaty, Buck informed me "one trip in there was enough to do him." It took us three hours to get back into the lake. If we'd had an empty boat, it would have been easier. But this time the boat was full of two hundred–pound fertilizer sacks of gator hides. Most of the time we spent dragging the boat around and over the logs. I was afraid we'd punch a hole in that boat 'cause Buck had made the bottom out of tomato crates. Then we'd have been in a mess. It made a good bottom, though.

When we returned to the road [Ingraham Highway] where we had left a Model A Ford, night was coming on, and we was tired. We loaded up and started down the rock road to town. Now in those days—in the '30s—just a few cars or trucks a week traveled this road during the spring of the year. We would leave the skeeter on the road, and most times it wasn't messed with, and we could get it started.[19] West Lake was about thirty miles from town, and it was eighteen miles of rocky road from Palm Hammock to West Lake. Sometimes it was very rough.

Having a history of being loggerheaded, I soon became too sleepy to drive; we stopped, and I tried to turn the driving over to Buck. Well now Mr. Buck wouldn't drive, but I was pretty sure he could. Laying down in the rocky road, I was soon asleep. I could have slept there all night, but Buck had right away built a fire. He made some strong coffee, woke me up, and handed me a can of it. "Drink that, and let's go," he said. Like I said, there was a woman in his life, and we got going toward town. Not much to that happening, but I often wondered whether he could drive or not. Years later he bought a brand new vehicle and drove that. I would have let a blind man drive that night.

The Yappos

I first heard the name Yappos when I was real young, from the old-timer deer hunters.[20] The landmarks are gone now, and it was always hard to get there. You had to go on foot or you could take a glade skiff at high water. There were gator holes back in there. At one time, the ancient Indians had camped there. The Seminole hunted there some when I did—but left little sign, as they only quick-camped and went on (as we did). The Yappo Strand was a bunch of rock humps that run from near the pinewoods west of Homestead. They ran three or four miles westerly, then they crossed the old Context Road [the Yappos cross the Context Road about four miles past the road's locked gate] and headed north westerly for a few miles. The Yappos are about eight miles long.

The humps were like a string of pearls through the prairie from the pinewoods. The Yappos was at one time a hogback—like the one from Grossman's Hammock toward the Shark River. Over the years the Yappos grew pine trees, maybe two to five on a clump. The pines on these islands were very big in diameter. Some years we took our skiffs in there or went in part way by glade buggy. If the water was low, we'd walk in. We did more walking by far than by glade buggy. Oman Barber said he had two glade buggies, and he pointed to his feet.

There was a time when a man in the Everglades could always see a smoke somewhere. When walking on long trips, you'd come across burns of different ages—like a patchwork quilt. This kept the glades alive with game and the hammocks green, and pretty too. The do-gooder people of this country seem to pick out a cause, and they think that people that don't follow suit are to be scorned. In 1928 or 1929, the University of Miami put up signs around the glades that said, "Fire destroys game and game cover." Some of these signs were fifteen feet by six feet and high off the ground so you could see them. One was on the road outside of Palm Hammock, and one was near Jenson's Pine four miles south of the Loop Road on the watershed. The signs also listed the trouble you was in if convicted of setting fires. I'm writing from memory, or lack of it, and might have some dates wrong—but I remember the signs.

After that, rambling men got afraid to burn. But in the case of this early effort to keep out fires—with so much drainage and without fires in the wet season to keep things down—the peat built up and zappo, the fire burnt all the pine trees off the Yappos in 1934 [when Glen says the peat built up, he means the organic matter and soils].[21] Without fires in the wet season, this country burns out to the bone and kills everything in the ground in the spring. In 1934, the peat burned for weeks—killing the wildlife and all the pine trees that grew on the Yappo islands. One seeing the Yappos now would not realize how they looked before the 1934 fire. Every island had large pines, some of the biggest ever seen in South Florida. Some of the bones from these pines lay there for years. All the sap and bark fell around the trees like a large cone that covered over fifteen feet. The sap cones eventually burnt, too, in 1962 in that big fire.

You can see the Yappos pretty plain about five miles off where the pinewoods used to be along the shallow Everglades west of Homestead. The Yappos are pretty plain there—lots of clumps. I called the middle part of the Yappos "Pine Island"—but there are probably as many humps called Pine Island in the lower Everglades as there are Lonesome Pines.[22] This Pine Island wasn't really an island but the center of the Yappos—a rocky willow slough that was broken up by small humps of pinewoods and hammocks. The shelf was a part of the Pine Island—it was a natural rock shelf that went out for about ten acres to the north.[23] The shelf was mostly flat, not broken up with pinnacle and well rocks, but it had some gator holes and lots of willows. It was so flat that the Piper Cubs used to land there. There were five gator holes along the shelf. It was on the northwest corner of Pine Island. We killed a few deer on the shelf. A hundred acres of sloughs cut into Pine Island.

In 1943 I was camped some five miles into the Yappo Strand in the middle of Pine Island on the Oak Tree Camp. Oaks had grown there since 1934, after the fire. We always walk-toted everything in over the rocks. Never used a glade buggy to go all the way to camp. That way only people from the air could see you. We'd put a tin shelter between two hardy oaks—so as to hide it from blowflies [Piper Cubs] and glade buggies. As no matter what you're doing—if you'll stay hid, try and keep your doings to yourself, never tell if you kill something or catch it—I'll guarantee you that there'll be more of it. No matter, that is to say, that was the way it was before blowflies. Nothing in the sawgrass lands was kept from them, they could see it all. But moving about from one section of the swamp to another helped.

I left home at night and jumped off at the edge of the glades and walked the five miles to this tin shelter on Oak Trees—as I did often.[24] Being tired when getting there, I just bedded down on some old bedding that we kept in a lard-can suitcase at the camp. There was also an old bed springs there and some cans and jars we kept hid. A water hole was right there in the camp that we kept dug out. Some kind of bad smell woke me at first light. Figuring it was a dead rat or something, I rolled over and covered my head, but the stench was just as bad. Not being ready to get up—but no matter which way I turned the smell was there. When I looked straight up at about good light, I saw a hoot owl was "being excused" on my shoulder—and that wasn't exactly shampoo or rose water in my hair either. The next night it seemed the thing to do was move the bed a few feet and sure enough just 'fore day the owl came home, but he didn't catch me unawares again. This camp cost not a penny and is still there, too.

Tommy Theus built a camp in a hammock some three miles westerly from Nixon Hammock in 1941 or 1942. This was one of the few camps we used in the Yappo country. Because the island had never burned since it had a wide band of rock around it, there was two feet of pure peat on top of the rocks at this camp. The hammock was in a rocky slough, a drift hammock. It was full of small oak trees, coco plum—very beautiful, full of native trees. Tommy loved to deer hunt and was noted for it. His camp was more substantial than most. It contained two buildings, one for sleeping and the other a kitchen. Tommy offered the use of his camp to me and Oman Barber. We took him up on his offer and would sometimes lay over there on some of our forays.

The camp's kitchen was stocked with canned goods, and Oman and I would leave some money under a can if we ate anything. On one trip we got caught in some bad, rainy weather and had to use some canned goods; that time we left five dollars. After we came back a few weeks later, we noticed that the money was gone. We thought Tommy had got it.

Oman and I were taking walking trips going westerly. There were several log roads that went down to the edge of the glade then. One was near the end of Mowry Street where it dead-ended at Loveland Road. This wagon road angled toward the glade—you could drive or get a ride and walk from there into the rocky shallow glades. Other fellows were also rambling this country, and one of these fellows could be put in the hellish category. Someone had found our camp (Oak Trees), which was a few miles further on from Tommy's, and had opened every canned good we had at our camp and left them that way—partly eaten. From then on, we buried all cans, bottles, and jars. Anyway, word got to us that this fellow had told others in town that for a long time he had been eating Tommy's groceries, and now Tommy had started leaving him money. A common man for sure.

Tommy's camp burned to the ground in 1962, a real hot fire—if I remember correctly. I figured this would happen since this island had never been burned before. The grass was sparse all around the hammock. The fire was so hot both the buildings were burnt away. The only thing that was left was the remainder of the water pump, and even the pump pipe had bent over like a hairpin from the extreme heat.

A camp I called Rat Camp also burned away. This camp was a mile or so west of Radius Rod Camp. I camped here only once or twice in the 1930s. As the water was high, I'd come by dugout canoe. There the rats had built up a pretty good family, as I found out. On the first night of the trip, I put my .22 sawed-off rifle in the bushes and did some hard sleeping on a gator-nest bed. Maybe those rats had the "miss-meal fever" because they were busy making a meal out of my gun stock that night. This didn't bother me too much, as they left enough for me to use and it wasn't no thing of beauty to start with. But to keep them from eating the rest of it, I laid it beside me the next night.

Since it was a warm night, with only a few mosquitoes and smoke on both sides of me, sleep come easy. I had learned not to sleep on my back because the snoring would wake me up. When I stepped on the rocks around the camp the next morning, my feet hurt so bad that I sat back down on the gator-nest bed. I looked at my feet, and the rats had eaten all the calluses off my feet. They bled very little, but I saw a jillion teeth marks, and I knew I had played hell again. I don't think that my feet ever got over that, they still hurt when thinking about it— "eaten alive." There is no feeling in a callus, had there been, I'm sure I would have quit feeding them rats in a hurry. Yes, I put my shoes on.

The Hide Trade

C H A P T E R 3

Tales of moody alligators lurking about in murky, humid swamps have always loomed large in Florida's narrative history, an almost necessary counterpoint to the state's orange-blossom veneer. William Bartram's decidedly fantastic encounter with one such reptile in 1794 ("Suddenly a huge alligator rushed out of the reeds, and with a tremendous roar came up, and darted as swift as an arrow under my boat, emerging upright on my lee quarter, with open jaws, and belching water and smoke that fell upon me like rain in a hurricane.") helped set the tone for at least another century.[1] By the late nineteenth and early twentieth centuries, an increasing number of gentlemen explorers, naturalists, and surveyors began to trickle down into the extreme southern part of the state. They conducted expeditions up the coastal rivers and into the interior swamps and marshes behind Cape Sable, the Ten Thousand Islands, and the new towns along the southeastern coasts. Their lively accounts and photographs appeared in such popular magazines of the time as *Harper's*

Weekly and *Scribner's,* and they began to offer readers a slightly more cautious profile of alligators and the men who sought them, allaying some of the topic's earlier melodrama.

Today when strolling the beautiful Anhinga Trail, one of Everglades National Park's most popular and accessible walks, the sight of dense huddles of camera-laden visitors usually signals the presence of an alligator just beyond the safety of the trail's elevated boardwalk. And this fascination is not difficult to understand. Alligators, whose short legs support a long, muscular torso and tail covered mostly with horny, rectangular scales, have changed little since the age of the dinosaurs. Like all reptiles, alligators are cold-blooded, so they spend the majority of their time lazily warming themselves along sunny embankments, although they become suddenly swift when lunging after prey—indiscriminately grabbing for any bird, fish, frog, turtle, or small mammal with their powerful, elongated jaws. It's not surprising that while documented cases of alligators attacking humans are quite rare, popular folklore of the South has often featured such incidents. A notable inclusion in this genre is Van Campen Heilner's 1922 "Death Struggle with an Alligator." Here Heilner, who waded into an Everglades pond to photograph a large alligator, dramatically recounts, ." . . I felt my right leg gripped in a frightful vise, and before I could cry out, I was dragged under that awful slime, down, down, with a pair of gruesomely human hands tearing at my legs. I struggled and kicked in agony. This death-lizard was killing me! I bethought me of my sheathknife and plunged it with all my might into what I judged was the monster's eye" (1922, 208).

Even after rifles were commonly used in alligator hunting, the men whose livelihood depended on selling the hides spent considerable effort physically wrangling alligators out of their caves, while avoiding their massive musculature and jaws. Gladesmen seemed to exhibit a cautious nonchalance toward this close contact, mixed perhaps with a healthy dose of respect. A story told to A. W. Dimock by his unnamed guide best illustrates this attitude:

One day when we was skinnin' on the island [in a lake north of Cape Sable], somehow the boat got away and drifted ashore. Will said he'd swim fer it providin' I'd stand by with the rifle and keep off the

'gators. Well, when he got most ashore I began to shoot all 'round
him and hollered to him to swim fast, thet the 'gators was after him.
He most busted hisself gettin' to shore and I near died laffin,' but he
jest walked off an' left me alone on thet island with a lot o' stinkin
carcasses 'till most the night the nex' day. I ain't usually 'fraid o'
'gators and would hev swum ashore, but this time they was too
damn thick and I reckon I must hev scared myself when I frightened
my partner. (1915, 119)

This studied indifference to the dangers of alligators undoubtedly
stemmed from necessity, as alligator hunting was essential to the cultural
fabric of the people living along the margins of the Everglades.

Gladesmen adapted their hunting to the region's annual cycles of
rain and drought, and importantly, to the economics of the trade. These
forces dictated all aspects of their livelihood: what size alligator to hunt,
the methods for hunting, how hides were prepared, and where they
were sold. While alligators were hunted throughout the year, the methods differed substantially according to the seasons. As described below,
when water levels were low in the glades alligators were hunted from
their caves (also called dens). When the prices were low, alligator hunters
supplemented their incomes by selling raccoon and otter pelts during the
winter months. During the rainy season and on cloudy days, the hunters
pursued their prey at night—from boats in the higher waters of the Everglades. As Glen Simmons describes, the market determined how gladesmen prepared the hides—whether only the soft belly skins were sold
(called "flatskins") or whether the thicker back part of the hide was also
removed (called "hornbacks") on smaller alligators.

The alligator hide trade became economically lucrative after the mid–
1800s, and this induced an increasing number of men into the backcountry lakes, marshes, and sloughs of the Everglades. Albert Reese, a
zoologist, explains in The Alligator and Its Allies that although the Civil
War created a market for alligator leather in the South, the hide's popularity really increased after 1869 (1915, 27). By the turn of the century,
Florida's alligator hide trade was well established, and the state represented the chief supplier of hides to tanneries throughout the East Coast.
Reese notes that Cocoa, Melbourne, Fort Pierce, Miami, and Kissimmee

An unskinned alligator at a camp on Bear Lake, spring 1936.

served as the most important centers for the trade. For instance, three firms in Kissimmee handled thirty-three thousand alligator hides in 1899 (Reese 1915, 27). Dimock also describes the trade during this period, estimating that the principal hide dealer on Florida's west coast was buying three or four hundred hides per day in 1898. According to Dimock, this enterprising dealer also "kept a schooner running to Key West with hides and returning with cargoes of salt, ammunition and grub" (Dimock 1926, 119). By 1902, tanneries in the United States produced approximately 280,000 skins annually, worth about $420,000, with 22 percent of the hides originating in Florida (Reese 1915, 28). As Glen describes in this chapter, he bought and sold hides in the 1930s and 1940s through a loose network of local buyers and other hunters. Any accumulated hides were then resold to one of the three large hide buyers in the state—with Glen either traveling to their locations or arranging for the hides to be picked up.

Until the 1940s, the price hunters received for hides increased only incrementally. For the year 1898, Dimock reports alligator hunters receiving from one dollar for hides measuring seven feet or more, to as little as ten cents a hide for those less than four feet long (1926, 119). Reese quotes a U.S. Bureau of Fisheries report that shows a gradual increase in price between 1891, when hide prices averaged sixty cents per skin, and 1902, when hides averaged ninety cents, with some worth two dollars (1915, 28). Approximately ten years later, Seminole Indians at Brown's "Boat Landing" in the Big Cypress Swamp received ten cents a foot for alligator hides up to eight feet long (Kersey 1975, 62). After alligators became more scarce in the 1920s, perhaps because of increased drainage efforts and several decades of overhunting, prices rose to between twenty-five cents for a three-foot hide to three dollars for a seven footer (Kersey 1975, 127). Glen received $2.50 to $3.00 for seven-foot hides during the 1930s. During this same period, a graduated price scale was commonly used (set prices were given for size ranges, rather than being priced by the foot), with skins more than seven feet long worth three dollars, six-foot hides worth two dollars, and five-foot hides worth one dollar. Sellers received fifty cents for four-foot hides and twenty-five cents for three-foot hornbacks.

Demand for alligator leather increased during World War II, and the prices for hides rose substantially. Glen also reports a shift in the way alligator hides were priced. Now hide buyers consistently priced the skins by the foot, with prices rising to as high as one dollar per foot.[2] The demand for hides also grew as fewer hunters participated in the trade. As Glen notes, meat rationing policies during the war years made fishing much more lucrative and also "kept some men out of the service." Therefore, fishermen who initially supplemented their income by hunting alligator and otter were able to fish full time. And of course, a large number of young men, including Glen, volunteered or were drafted into military service.

Hunting alligators in South Florida also became slightly more difficult after 1939, as state laws were passed which specifically limited alligator hunting in a number of Florida counties. These statewide acts imposed sanctions and limitations (for alligator and crocodile hunting, the transportation of hides, or the selling of live alligators and crocodiles and their eggs) based upon each county's population size. For instance, hunting seasons, rather than outright bans, were established for smaller counties. Yet separate legislation—specifically Florida House Bill No. 1839 signed in June of 1939—completely outlawed the capture, injury, or killing of alligators and crocodiles within Dade County. Conviction under this law imposed stiff sanctions, with fines ranging from one hundred to five hundred dollars or imprisonment of up to six months in the county jail. While this law represented a further obstacle to hunters in the southern Everglades, it was somewhat difficult to enforce since alligator hunting remained legal in adjacent Monroe County for another decade.

Gladesmen in the Everglades, as well as the rest of Florida, used two techniques for hunting alligators: pole-hunting and fire-hunting. Hunting alligators from their caves during the day, usually during the dry season, was referred to as pole-hunting. Traditionally, the hunter would wade carefully into the alligator's pond and then ram a long cypress pole with a large hook attached to its end into the alligator's cave. When the alligator bit the hook, the hunter pulled him out of the cave—with a great degree of effort and struggle—and then struck him with an ax. An iron rod was also used to force the alligator forward in the cave. Dimock describes this process, saying, "One of the hunters thrust a thin iron rod through the soil until it stuck the 'gator, which soon poked its head out of the cave, another caught his hook in the jaw of the reptile, while the third hunter smashed its skull with an axe" (1926, 273). As the photographs that accompany Dimock's chapter "An Alligator Hunter in the

Making" illustrate, this process was labor intensive and required at least two men.

The method of pole-hunting used by Glen and his contemporaries differed somewhat from the process described by Dimock and others, such as Charles Cory (1896). Although called "pole-hunting," hunters in Glen's era largely abandoned the pole-hook method. Instead of dragging the alligators from their caves and killing them with axes, Glen and his contemporaries used various methods of agitating the alligators until they came out of their caves. Then the gators were shot with .22 rifles. The use of more modern rifles put an end to the earlier belief that the alligator's hide acted as a protective shield from which bullets would simply bounce off (Glasgow 1991, 28). As Cory explains, "The old idea that a rifle-ball would glance from the skin of an alligator does not apply to modern weapons. If a rifle-ball strikes fairly it will penetrate the skin without difficulty and will sometimes pass completely through the body" (1896, 69). Glen suggests that earlier pole-hunters also used axes, instead of rifles, to conserve their ammunition. He further notes that a variety of circumstances (such as a scarcity of ammunition, the need to avoid detection, or in cases when the alligator was fairly small) led more modern hunters to dispose of their prey with a sharp hatchet or pocket knife. After abandoning the pole-hook method, alligator hunters were also able to hunt alone.

For more than a century, Florida gladesmen were famed for their ability to lure alligators from their underwater caves by imitating the grunting sounds made by baby gators. Cory describes this process saying, "After two or three grunts, as it is termed (although the call does not resemble a grunt at all), one or more alligators would rise to the surface and lay looking at us for a moment. The hunter has to shoot quickly under these circumstances, as the alligator soon discovers the deception and will not come up a second time for any amount of grunting" (1896, 66). The sound begins with a deep rumble formed at the back of the throat, which is punctuated with moments of silence and shaped with a slightly higher note at the end of each call. Glen employed a variation of this technique and actually grunted against the iron rod used for prodding the alligator from its cave. Even with these tricks, pole-hunting took a lot of patience as there was a certain sameness to much of the task: hours of kneeling beside an alligator's cave, waiting for it to emerge with only the companionship of mosquitoes and horseflies to break the solitude.

Popular wisdom of a couple of centuries back cautioned that the use of fire was the only hope for a hapless wanderer who unexpectedly encountered an alligator—as fire was the only thing these reptiles feared (Glasgow 1991, 14). This belief may account for fire-hunting's initial appeal, a hunting method that relied on the use of flaming torches to spot the alligators at night. Alligator eyes reflect a red glow when hit with the light from fire or from other sources, making them easy targets on dark evenings. Gladesmen fire-hunted from ponds, rivers, and sloughs during the wet season when the water was too high in the marshes to walk comfortably, as well as on moonless nights during the rest of the year.

The use of torches became obsolete in the late 1800s when hunters began using powerful carbide-burning lights worn strapped to their heads, called a bull's-eye lantern. These lanterns emitted a powerful single beam, which blinded or froze the alligators—similar to the effect of a car's headlights upon animals crossing a dark road. Dimock participated in a fire-hunt at the turn of the century and describes wearing a bull's-eye lantern, saying, "Because of lack of padding or a skull too thin the lantern bruised my head and blistered my brains, but the pictures painted that night remain bright in my memory" (1915, 116). After the alligator was located with the light, it was then shot, and a gator hook was used to drag it toward the boat. Once beside the skiff, the hunter braced the alligator's head over the side of the boat, then used a hatchet to cut through the animal's spinal cord right below the skull, the spot Glen refers to as the "sticker."

When I was growing up, alligators were thought to be a problem, and most gators were killed just for sport. I would guess that less than half of these gators were ever sold, although at most every home there were gator hides, salted and rolled up, ready in case a hide buyer came along. From modern man's beginnings in the glades country, until now, more gators have been killed for the hell of it than were ever sold—and it may always be that way. But when your teeth rotted out and there was no money to fix them, it hurt when somebody killed your "money" just for the fun of it.

Many deer hunters' dogs have been killed and eaten by gators, and this made the boys so mad. It's a wonder that any gators survived the thoughtless gator killing. I heard one man say that a gator in their camp would lay out on a rock nearby and had become used to the men coming and going for water. But only God knows why they got the idea of pouring gasoline on that gator and setting it on fire. And they did. He got back in the cave, and the next day he was gone.

Men that would do a thing of that kind are not understandable to me. Besides, what better than a gator to keep a water hole hollowed out.[3] The next time they came back to their camp, the well was dry, and the mud cracked open. I've had men tell me things they've done without any shame in their voices—such as shooting the camp gator to keep him from eating the fish. The fish wouldn't have been there without that gator keeping the hole open in the first place. I was told by another that he and some city boys had dynamited a sea cow [manatee] that had come up one of the canals. They didn't need the meat. I believe that men and boys, when two or more are together, will do some hellish acts they wouldn't do by themselves. A wonder to me is that they seem to seek me out to tell me these things, but maybe they would tell it anyway to anybody, as most men have a common streak.

Another time when I was walking along the strands of the Wink Eye Slough, enough sign was seen that I knew a big gator was near. I saw a couple of buzzards fly out of a willow patch. Of course that kind of took the starch out of me since it made me think someone had beat me to the gator I was looking for and had left its carcass for the buzzards. Although I saw no signs that anyone had been around, a bad smell made me start looking for that carcass. But instead of finding the gator, I came across an expensive looking black-and-tan hound, with a collar on it, floating high in the slough.

People were wildcat hunting in those days, and this wildcat dog had been caught by a gator. The gator had squeezed the poor dog so badly that its liver was sticking out of its belly. This dog had tried to make it across the gator's path, but it must have run into some vines that slowed him down. That's when that big sambo gator caught him. When I found him, the dog was about rotten enough for the gator to shake it into pieces small enough to swallow. I sold that gator's hide (a twelve-foot hide, which means he was ten feet in the flesh). No one ever mentioned that missing dog to me, and I said nothing. I felt that it was better not to say anything about something like that because it might cause a gator-hunting rampage to start and there were already too many Sunday hunters. I had a better use for them gators than to see 'em rot in the canals.

Searching for Gators

In the far south end of the state, there are two kinds of gator holes: ones in the peat and those in the rock. In the rockland, fires often burn out all the peat and grass buildup that fills solution holes. A gator will then make a cave out of one of these cleaned-out rock overhangs. Gators only dig and clean out their caves when the water is up enough to suit them. Sometimes these caves get crusty dry, and the gator will lay in the shade until the rain starts. Even after hunting a particular hole, it was a good idea to check back later—since you never knew when another gator would take up residency. Some of these holes were so desirable that they were good for five, six, or more visits a year—especially those in a long slough.

You can spot a gator hole that has an occupied cave by the richness of the plant growth and the color of things. If you spot a higher clump of sawgrass across the glade, usually there is a gator hole underneath it. You could even see the bird nests that are around an active hole from a long way off. Blackbirds and little green herons always seem to nest near a gator hole.

Glen peering into a gator hole in the rocky glades west of Homestead, 1950s.

After a few years of hunting the area, I knew where most every cave was in South Florida. You kind of keep track of where you've been last and figure out your walking or poling route from the past trip. As you spend time traveling this country, you begin to figure out the best way to go to hit the most caves (a straight, crooked line, so to speak).

There were many areas that I often hunted, such as along the Reef, in the mangrove country, the Fox Lakes, and Cuthbert Lake. The Taylor Slough, especially in the ditches of the Madeira Farms, was some of the richest pole-hunting country there was. There were gator holes all up and down that slough. It seemed to replenish itself. You could take a gator out of a hole there, come back three months later, and more than likely there'd be another one in there. Sometimes it did get overhunted though, since it was closer to the road. The Indians especially liked to hunt here. Before the park, we'd also hunt right there in Palm Hammock. We knew where all the old caves were in there. Since this was a protected area because the Women's Club had a park there, we would have to be careful to avoid the warden.[4]

But it's such a big country, sometimes you didn't get back to the same place in the same year. East and west of the pinewoods, everywhere there was gator holes. But that was before the Corps of Engineers put the [drainage] canals in here and cut the gators off, so to speak. Then they got in those canals and stayed there until someone killed them. A hundred-dollar gator killed for a few dollars worth of meat.

Having visited the same caves year after year, I knew just how each cave run in a particular hole.[5] Gators would be in the same place, just about all the time, except when the water was real high, then the younger and maiden gators looked for new caves. They would have a cave close to their nesting area and a main cave. Sometimes the babies would be in a cave off a short ways from where she was mating. Sometimes their caves would fill up with peat, or leaves and things, fill about half up, and they'd bury down under that and make a cave. But a lot of those holes didn't have much of a cave under the rock.

For many miles west of Homestead, near the Yappos, there are gator holes that we used to call "well rocks" since they were so deep and pretty. Some of these holes probably were springs at some point, as a few still bubbled in the '30s. Gators have lived in these rocky holes for thousands of years and have caused them to erode. As I have no scientific knowledge, I can only use a lifetime of firsthand observation to figure out what happened. The type of rock hereabouts is constantly being eaten away, breaking off, and being eroded. Gators live in these large cracks, which act as caves, that extend away from these holes.

The caves in the rock holes were under water except in extremely dry times. When it's dry, a gator hunter often has to contortion himself into these rock holes and get down with the gator. First you have to slip up on the hole and then quietly work your way back into the small cave until you spotted the gator. Sometimes, another person would hold onto the man's legs who was in the cave—that way he could be yanked out real quick in case the gator started after him.

Oman Barber and I were hunting one such rock cave, which had a big opening on the side and some small holes into the top. The water was so low that there was no water in the cave. We could see the gator's tail through the top hole but nothing else. Oman went in through the big opening, carrying his .22, as I watched the show from one of the overhead openings. He slowly bent and crouched his way into the cave, trying to get to a place where he could shoot the gator behind its head. Just as he fired, the large gator quickly whipped around. Oman reacted backward, his back making a hard contact with the sharp rock walls. For the rest of the trip, his back was bloody as if he'd toted a deer a long way. I saw that show but didn't laugh about it until I got by myself—but I sure wanted to. I've got many snickers out of it since. Oman told that story later sitting around a campfire, but it didn't come out like I seen it.

On another trip hunting in the rocklands along the road to Grossman's Hammock, the water was sure enough high, and the road was under water. The big tomato farmers could only see the tops of their vines sticking out of the water. They had taken a chance farming the large, deep glade a few miles east of Grossman's (now called Lake Chekika).[6] The water got too deep for the Model A so we jumped off with two glade skiffs and poled the last mile or so down the rock road and turned south into the Taylor Slough. We camped on a living site of some old-time Indians. At the time, this site had never been dug in, it being covered with pottery.

At daylight, on a muggy morning in November, a gator started to bellow about a quarter mile away. We were cooking breakfast. I laid a stick toward the sound, as we often did, so we could go there later. Well, my partner and me were both jumpy people, but he (and I won't say his name to save him the embarrassment) right away decided that the sound was really some game wardens trying to start an outboard motor. He said, "There coming after us!" He was as nervous as a flagpole sitter in a hurricane and was trying to see out them bushes. Sometimes a gator starts to bellow slowly, *uh-uh-uh-uh-uh-uh*, and it sounds like pulling on a small outboard motor. Anyway I'll never forget it.

It wasn't as if he hadn't heard many gators bellow over the years. But he had just woke up and didn't think straight for a few minutes. I never mentioned this story to him as long as he lived. This old slough was made by the rushing water from the north. This slough was hard on a boat bottom as the sharp rocks could be near the surface in places. And with my lack of memory, I hit many rocks every time it was glade skiffed. For thousands of years, the rushing water cut these sloughs and boy did it jump around, taking the easy way, sometimes in every direction but north. One could travel it many years, walking when dry and glade skiffing when wet—and learning something different every time. Some places had been lakes of such a depth of marl that it could be plowed with a mule and farmed. One lake bed of one hundred acres or more that bordered the pines just west of Loveland Road (217th Avenue) at 344th Street is still being farmed. Before bulldozers, this area was rich in gator holes.

Pole-hunting

Before I started hunting, men used to hunt gators with a long pole that they'd cut out of a cypress tree. They'd attach an iron hook to the end of the pole and then walk down into the gator pond and stick the pole into the gator's cave. The gator would then bite the hook, and the hunter would pull him out and hit him in the sticker [back of the neck] with a hatchet. When they used the pole, the hunter had to get down into those muddy caves and reach into them with a pole. The stench from the dead fish during low water would slow your breathing.

This way of hunting was messier than using an iron rod, which is how I've mostly done it. You didn't have to get into the pond when you were hunting with an iron rod. The rod was three-eighths of an inch in diameter and was six or eight feet long. You pushed the rod through the ground to find the gator's cave. And of course you knew how the cave run most the time. Sometimes you'd find a new cave—or one that is new to you. Then you had to feel it out from the start to the back, till you hit him with that rod. Most caves are straight. When you hit him, you pulled the rod out just a little bit cause he might bite it and twist the rod right up (then you can't get your rod out). Some of them are that strong. So you pull it up a little bit off him. And grunt a few times on the rod. Then you got to slip to the mouth of the cave or where you could at least see the mouth of the cave. We'd also always put a feeler inside the cave, a big stalk of sawgrass or a willow top, and

A cypress gator-hunting pole rests on a Model A glade buggy, 1940. This glade buggy had a separate gas tank attached to the hood that allowed the car to be started with gasoline and then run on kerosene.

when he come out, he'd move that. When you saw that feeler move, you'd know to be ready. Pick up your gun and shoot him—pop him in the back of the head.

When hunting during the day, surprising the gator when it was on the bank was the easiest. You'd try to slip up there, from down wind, and find the gator laying on the bank and try to get him before he went into his cave—which are many times under water. Most every gator in this country will lay out on the bank all day long. But if he heard anything at all or smelled anything, he'd come off the bank and get in the cave before you got there. If he did that, you knew you weren't going to be able to kill him as easily as if you had caught him on the bank. If you got him on the bank, you could slip up there and shoot him in the most vulnerable place to kill him [in the eye or the ear] with a .22 rifle—or a larger caliber if you was also deer hunting.

If you were walking on peat, and he went into his cave, he knew where you was all the time. And that gator ain't going to come out of his cave for awhile. Most of the time, he'd just stay down there. So I'd try to get across from the cave and sit there for awhile, real still, for about thirty minutes. If he didn't come out on his own, you'd prod him a few times with the iron rod by sticking the rod through the ground above the cave until it reached him—then make a few grunts like a baby gator. Most times he'd come out. You'd know he was coming when you saw a blubber [bubble] coming out of the mouth of the cave. That don't mean the gator was putting out any air, although they sometimes did release some air before coming up. But a blubber means he's moving—since there is air in the ground, and he is forcing it out. When you saw that blubber, or the feeler in the cave moved, you knew he's a-coming out, and you was ready for him.

But they weren't all that easy to kill. Sometimes you'd have trouble with them. Sometimes they wouldn't come out, and it would take much longer. I've waited a long time. A lot of people might think I don't know what I'm talking about, but if a large gator slips in his cave before you get there—and he don't move and use up his oxygen, just stay still—he could stay there quite a few hours. When the water was up, the gator generally doesn't have any air in there. God almighty, seems like I waited half the night or half the day on some of them gators. But if you could keep him moving, he'd have to come out sooner—since he's using up his air.

If you was walking and you didn't get him out by dark, you'd build a fire near there, and he'd generally come out at dark. If he just stuck his nose out for air, it was common for people to shoot them in the end of the nose. Then he'd have to come up for air. Sometimes we shot them under water (by putting the gun under the water). But that would ruin your gun after a dozen times or so—although I did that more than I should have. When the skeeters are all over you, you wanted to do something to get him up in a hurry.

Since you couldn't get your rod through in a rock cave, you just had to sit there quietly and wait it out—not shake the ground or anything. You could wait for him as far away as fifty feet or more and still shoot him. While I was waiting, I'd grunt from time to time, like a baby gator. Generally that would bring them out. But them old gators, they were smart. I think they were smarter in my time. There wasn't a gator in this country that hadn't had a bad experience with man. There had been gator hunters years ago; the gators no doubt got some wildness from what happened then.

* * *

My daddy used to say "damn a boy," and sometime after he was killed I knew why. I was hard at hunting gators and at the time was pole-hunting because the water was too low to glade skiff. A young lad we called Snag, for a chipped tooth, would sometimes tag along 'cause his folks knew it was good for him. He liked it anyway and wasn't much trouble, for about a ten-year-old yearling boy. I came to a rocky hole, I knew by the drag sign that more'n apt an eight-footer was there and hoped to catch the gator up or laying out. I motioned to the boy to stay back, and he did. It turned out that the gator was in his cave.

I hunkered down in the grass, where the area around the cave could be seen, and waited—grunting like a baby gator. Soon I saw a blubber, and he began rising slowly to the top—what Oman Barber called "ciphering." About that time, for some reason I never knew, this boy come a-running at a breakneck speed. And maybe he couldn't, but he sure didn't stop. He landed in the hole right on top of where the gator was coming up. That gator was more scared than Snag was. After that I knew that gator wasn't coming out till after dark, so we left him till later. He never told me why he jumped in that hole, but something had him traveling like Frazier's bullet. He hardly stayed in the water long enough to get wet. I didn't say what I felt like saying, and I'm glad I didn't. What's the use?

* * *

When you do find a gator, there are only three places to shoot him. Where you shot him depended upon where he came out, how he raised his head, and where you were. If you was behind him, you'd shoot him in the back of the head—and it was really over. That was really death. If he come up sideways, you'd shoot him in the ear. You put it in that little hole where his ear is, ain't much bigger than a .22 bullet. And if he'd come up facing you, you'd shoot him in the top of the eye. That's death. But never shoot one between the eyes, if you're on the level with him—'cause it will just bounce right off, and the bullet will be off in the wide blue yonder.

In 1935, I poled my glade skiff to the Bill Ashley Camp near Oyster Bay on the Joe River. It was a fifteen-mile pole to the camp; from camp we'd walk-hunt looking for otters, gators, and deer. We often used the Bill Ashley Camp because we could hide our glade skiffs there and avoid any visitors for two or three weeks while we were in the swamp. This area was made up of some of the richest wildlife marsh I'd ever seen. Ducks, coots, curlews, flintheads, and cooters were abundant. I was by myself on this two-week trip and found almost anything I wanted to eat in the meat line.

The ground was spongy, which means that an alligator can feel you coming and may slip into his cave. When the conditions are like this, a gator can almost feel you breathing. When they are in their caves, some of the big gators are hard to make rise. On this particular trip, after grunting awhile at the gator hole, I gave up and made tracks to the camp since I wanted to return by dark.

If you grunt a gator and he don't come out, he'll leave after it's dark to go to another hole or creek. Sometimes a gator will leave and travel a long ways. Most of the time you could trail him and get him in the morning. For some reason, this gator followed me down my trail, which was about a mile to camp. I guess it was easy traveling. Maybe he was trying to save me the trouble of toting a twelve-foot hide to the camp. I was lying under my skeeter bar with a small tarp stretched between two cabbage palms. About midnight, I heard the dried cabbage fronds and sticks breaking in the path toward my camp. The night was pitch black, and I didn't have a light.

I woke up and thought, "God Almighty, that gator is coming right toward me." And knowing that he didn't want me was little help. Then all of the sudden, he stopped—about fifteen feet from where I was lying. He must have sensed me because he stayed still for about ten minutes. My heart was trying to jump out. Then with a wild rush he headed for the river and he knocked down the foot end of my skeeter bar. When I heard him move, I rushed out the other end of the skeeter bar and ran smack dab into a cabbage palm tree. Then, the wonderful sound of that sambo gator hitting the river. To my knowledge that salt-burner was never skinned by me.[7]

The smartest thing a gator hunter could do was kill the sambo gators 'cause they try to take over the swamp. Eating young gators, often killing the weaker males, and fighting—cutting and tearing holes that damage the hides. They just want a few females around. The population increases when the big male gators are killed off—as more young'uns grow up that wouldn't have.

Fire-hunting

We fire-hunted at night from a glade skiff in the ponds, lakes, and other waterways in the glades and mangrove country. We also fire-hunted from the car, looking into the canals and ditches along the roads. At night, I'd use a carbide light, the bull's-eye lantern (until 1947). It made a longer light, and it just suited me so much better than an electric light—and it was cheap (and that was important in those times).

The road to the Keys was being put on the old railroad bed from Homestead to Key Largo in about 1943. At about the Woodall Rock Pit, which was seven miles south of Florida City, the road was blocked off. A night watchman was stationed there to turn any traffic back that might get that far, as there was road-building equipment on ahead to the south. But we had good relations with the watchman, and he let us come and go at will during the night—in exchange for some alligator meat to feed his family. We had that road to ourselves for the next ten miles or so. At that time, there were many gators in the old railroad ditches as far as the Glades Station.[8] From the Glades Station to Jew-fish Creek, there were also thousands of crocodiles—mostly young (from 1905 to 1943). A perfect place for them as they used the railroad bed and ditches to raise their young. To nest, they would simply lay their eggs in the railroad bed. A man walking with a light from the Glades Station to Jewfish Creek could see upward of a thousand crocs—mostly yearlings. When US 1 was put on the railroad beds, the crocs came up on the road and were run over at night—some of these were skinned, but most were ruined and wasted. The glory days for the railroad crocs were over with the coming of the highway on the railroad bed.

But man never used a better light for hunting gators than a bull's-eye lantern. They burned carbide and when adjusted right would burn for about three hours on two or three small lumps of carbide, about a half inch in diameter. All through the 1930s a two-pound can of carbide could be bought for fifty cents—this would last for several sets of dark nights. The bull's-eye light had a lens or glass that was about a half inch thick in the middle, oval, and thinner to the edges. This light was a little heavy, but good and cheap to use. The regulator was worn at the hip, while a hose ran from it to the lamp, which attached to your head.

When we were hunting from the Keys road, we were using a 1929 Model A Ford that had a waterproofed, chicken-wire, cotton, and tow-sacking roof (at least it was waterproof in earlier days). I was fire-hunting out the open window with the bull's-eye lantern. After smelling smoke, we discovered that the light had been turned up too high and had caught the roof on fire. I had built a mosquito smoke out of our automobile. We doused it with canal water, but the smell lasted much longer. If everyone had done as many damn fool things as me, it's doubtful the world could stand it.

*   *   *

When fire-hunting the lakes at night, you'd have to sit down in the skiff and paddle. This way you'd be on about level with them gators, and it was more steady. The pole could scare a gator if it hit a rock, and the bottom is rocky in some waters. But if you was by yourself, you'd have to lay the paddle down and pick up your gun without making any noise (I'd lay the paddle on some sort of padding on the bottom of the boat). When I got the skiff close enough, I'd shear off to the right of the gator just a little 'cause I shot to the left. I'd try to get within ten feet of him. 'Cause when you got your eye to the gator, sometimes you can't be sure which way he's laying when it's dark and all you can see is one eye. Though, most the time you could tell which way he's laying. Shoot him in the eye or in the ear.

A gator lies in the water at night. Seldom are they on land around here 'cause they are laying there listening trying to get something to eat. They generally bump around the edge of the shore a lot looking for snakes, rats, rabbits, coons, and such. The light usually will hold him—if it's a calm night, and he ain't too gun shy. But a lot of gators got foxy, and you couldn't get up to them—they'd been shot at or something. When you go to shoot him, he'd pull his head down or something. But, for the most part, they'd stay up if it was a calm night and if you hadn't made any noise getting up to him.

They will generally hold fire after awhile—but you'd have to leave them if they wouldn't.[9] They would go down and stay for a while, and you'd be looking for him with your carbide light. If you can't get him soon, then you might as well go on around and try to get him tomorrow night. I always leave some, and that was good in a way.

When I was fire-hunting, I'd leave right after dark and hunt till daylight. Then I'd sleep a little while. Course then you had to skin your gators in the morning. People got where they really knew their onions—they could skin them fast!

After I shot the little gators, four or five feet long, I'd drag them into the boat. We always had a gator hook with us—if he went to the bottom, you had to feel around for him and lift him into the boat with the hook. But for the most part, if you put that bullet where its supposed to be, he'll stay there till you get to him. The gator will just turn over on his back floating on the top of the water. Then you could reach him and catch him with your hand. You'd pull the head over the boat and chop him or cut him in the sticker with your knife. Once when I was up the North River by myself for a few nights during the 1930s, I shot a nine-footer and was going to cut him in the sticker with a hatchet—since shooting them sometimes only knocks them out. I pulled the gator's head into the boat, and as always, threw my leg over the gator to hold him in place. That night the hatchet was just out of reach, and so I picked up my .22 to shoot him in the sticker. As I was pulling the trigger, the gator flounced, which caused the bullet to ricochet into my leg. It burnt some and went in between the knee and hip. Using the point of the ripping blade, the bullet came out. It amounted to nothing but was sore for awhile.

Sometimes we'd have a boatload of gators, so we'd stake them out. We'd throw them overboard and put up a stake and then get them in the morning. Also, if he's big, you don't want to bring him into the boat 'cause he'd load you down. Sometimes we'd drag the big ones up by an old stump or something so we could find him the next morning. It wouldn't take more than two or three big ones to load your boat down, and you wouldn't want to do that.

Once when I was hunting with Buck Rohrer, we staked out a number of gators and came back to get them in the morning. When we pulled them up from under the water, one was missing. We were pretty sure another gator had gotten him. He was a short, only four feet long. On the next night, Buck and I killed an eleven-foot gator. When we opened him up the missing gator was inside. He had swallowed him head first. The hide had deteriorated so badly we couldn't use it. After that, I always put the shorts in the boat with me.

All the rivers and lakes could be hunted by glade skiffs, but the quicker you learned to stay out of some of them the better. For after the 1920s, most creeks, canals, and lakes could be reached by motorboat, and they were. From way back, men could hunt West, Cuthbert, and Long Lakes by way of Alligator Creek. The motorboat boys could cover a lot of territory quickly, and they'd clean out the gators. These motorboat boys would stop near the mouth of Alligator Creek, Bear Lake, and the East Cape Canal to do the skinning. After poling a glade skiff all night and having little to show for it, I'd come across those stinking carcasses, and I knew it was time to hit shallow water.

So glade skiffers had to stick to the gator country that the launches couldn't get into—you just couldn't compete when pushing a pole boat. After this fact of life entered my slow-working head I was better off. The best lakes for skiffers were Big Cattail and Little West Lakes.[10] These required lots of hand labor to get to and so weren't used by motorboaters.

During the war years when fish were selling good the hunting pressure on these waterways eased up—so the glade skiffers had a better chance. Many men who once hunted gators started fishing to dodge the draft. Fish had reached the best price ever, and the demand was good as meat was rationed and expensive. Black mullet brought ten cents per pound at Flamingo; snapper and red fish brought ten cents; trout brought twenty cents; jewfish and drum brought one cent a pound. Then there was a lot less competition in the gator lakes and rivers.

Skinning and Stretching

We would either skin a gator flat or hornback a lot of smaller ones—according to what the buyer needed. If we were pole-hunting or walk-hunting, we'd try to skin them on the spot. First, I'd pop his back open with a pocketknife, just behind the hind legs. Then I'd stick my knife into his backbone—he's dead, but his reflexes will cause him to rear up and break his own back, most times. When his back was broken, I'd then run a gator-rod fern or a willow branch down his back to take all the wiggle out of him.[11] You'd have to strip the leaves off the fern rod

Gator hides hanging at Fishhook Carter's camp on Canal Point, near Lake Okeechobee, 1939.

and then run the rod up to his head and then down toward his tail. Then you could skin him, 'cause this relaxed his involuntary muscles. If you didn't take the wiggle out of him with the fern, his muscles would twitch for half the day, and his hide would draw up to where you could damage the hide when you was skinning him. After he was relaxed, I could skin him right away and put his skin in my sack. If we were coming back to the same spot the next day, we could drop the gator overboard and skin him later. But it ain't too smart coming and going the same way.

At one time we just left the carcasses on the bank and let the buzzards eat them. Then after the law got so bad, with airplanes flying, I would hide the carcasses. A lot of times I'd stick them in the caves or cover them up with brush. If you can keep something out of sight from a buzzard, it will just wilt down.

*   *   *

When you hornback a gator, you take the whole hide—including the feet and sometimes the head. The buyer wanted the head on some of the smaller ones to put on a pocketbook or something. Then I'd leave the head on the hide and rip him right down the belly, one time, and take everything else [both the back and the softer belly skin]. When hornbacking a gator you want to save the feet—the skin is pulled off his feet and the toenails left on the hide. It ain't as slow as you think it is once you get on to it—especially if you use your bare feet to help work the hide off.

On the small ones, you could take your pocketknife and cut the skull out the top of his head because it is too thick to save the whole thing—you had to cut out part of the brain cap. If it was a four- or five-footer, you'd have to take a chisel with you and chisel out the brain cap when you got back to camp. Then you had to put some salt in there. When you got through, you had a hide with the whole gator there. They made pocketbooks with the head on them for years—that was the way they opened the pocketbook, with the head. Things were tacky back in them years.

If the hide buyer told you he wanted so many hornbacks—you know at such a length, maybe need a hundred three-foot hornbacks—then that's what you'd do. You'd fix them like that. If he wanted the head on, you'd get a little bit more money. Sometimes thirty-five cents apiece or more.

When making a flatskin, in the early days, they would cut the gator just below the horns on its back.[12] We called them horns but they call them scutes now—them things on the back, the little bones. We'd rip them around on each side just below the horns. Then when you got down to the tail part of the gator, we'd cut him below the fins. Some people got to ripping them so low—'cause they were easier to skin and took less salt and didn't weigh as much—that the hide buyers and the tanneries didn't want them. Ripping the hide too low and then trying to stretch the hide was what I called "shoestringing" it. The hide buyers then made you put a whole row of horns on each side of the hide— that assured them that they got the whole hide. It wasn't too bad either. When I got to the long fin on the tail, I'd open that up with a sharp knife. That would make a pretty fan out of it. We called it fan-tailing them.

Lot of times you didn't have no water to rinse him after you skinned him. Although that would be a good idea. Sometimes there would be a little blood on them, but that didn't hurt anything. But sometimes they were too nasty 'cause they had messed on themselves when you skinned them. You keep your foot on his belly when you're skinning him, and you're squeezing stuff out of him. Then we'd try to wash him—'cause it smells so bad. But a lot of times we had no water, during the dry times. And in the dry times, the water might be nastier than the hide.

I've found many things inside a gator when I've skinned them. In larger gators, I'd sometimes find their mouths full of decaying minnows—hundreds of them, they probably swam in or were sucked to their death. I've also seen gators with so many feathers in them that they couldn't stay under water. The rest of the bird would digest but the feathers just built up.

Best thing to do when you got back to camp at night was to salt them hides and roll them up kind of lightly. Then you let them stay there, maybe an hour or so, to take salt. Then you would stretch them, by hanging them over something like a clothesline or limb. When they were being stretched, all that water would run out of them at night.

The way we stretched most of them was to nail the lip around a stick or something with a small nail. This prevented the hide from tearing when we stretched it. Then we'd nail both ends of the gator's hide to a pole. I often carried a pole with me that I used all the time for stretching the hides. The weight of the gator would stretch it, and the next morning it would be sagging quite a bit, and it would be stretched. And that was all you had to do to stretch him. If you really pulled on it, you would be liable to break something. Then you'd lose it. Some buyers might not buy it. You had to make sure and check your hides every week or two—otherwise the maggots might get started, the hide would turn red from too much salt, or if the water got on them it might cause slippage of the scales.

Many hides were lost because of neglect or lack of a ready market. The best way to keep hides for a long period, as backwoods people didn't have freezers, was to pickle them in barrels of brine. Later in the '50s, freezers became common and that was the best way. I would salt the hides, lightly dry them, salt them again, and then freeze them.

*   *   *

Common men used to say that gators will stretch an extra inch to the foot. But really, a twelve-footer will stretch more than a foot—he'll stretch to over thirteen feet sometimes. But a little gator won't stretch an inch to the foot. The bigger the gator, the more it will stretch.

People would try to stretch their hides just as long as they could. They'd try to make a seven-footer out of a six. Then they expect you to buy it. Or they'd try to pull it down on your measuring board to reach the next mark. But if the hide bounced back to below the measurement, after they let it go, they weren't going to get it. It had to stay at that mark. Some of them would fuss at me when I was buying hides [Glen bought hides from other hunters to sell to dealers, as he discusses below], so I'd just reach down and wap off some of the tail with a knife. I'd say, "Are you satisfied now? That's all I'm going to get out of it, and that's all you're going to get out of it." And that's the way it was. Some of these old people around Homestead, they'd have one or two hides, and they'd think, by God, they was just going to get rich off them. Well, I guess you can't blame them. But, I was honest and made very little on a hide. I sold to a lot of different men in my life, and I never had any trouble. If it didn't make it, I wouldn't make any fuss about it. I'd take that lower mark.

During the '30s, if you could find a market, the price stayed at $2.50 to $3.00 for a seven-foot clear skin. Even if the hide was any length over seven foot and was clear and perfect, the price was the same. A six-foot brought two dollars, five-foot a dollar, four-foot brought fifty cents or a dollar. We got thirty-five cents for three-foot hornbacks. Of course, many skins were sold for less. These prices were about average of what the hunters got. After the middle of the war years, they started pricing hides by the foot. At one point [in the 1960s], the prices went as high as five dollars a foot—if you could find the right buyer. I remember in the mid-forties you could sell three-footers for a dollar each.

A "button hide" is a hide over six or seven feet that has flintlike flat pieces in the belly skin.[13] Most gators over five feet develop neck buttons, but these do not count off of the price. It's the belly buttons, the hard spots that won't bend, that ruined the skin since it kept it from being pliable. In the early days, button hides were worthless. Later, after 1935, the button hides were worth half price—they said they could use them to make suitcases. But they had a hard time trying to tan them. William McKinley Osceola told me that the Indians could tell by the sign around a gator cave about how long a female had lived there. If they thought she'd been there a long time—like fifteen years of nesting—they knew she'd probably be buttoned, and they would leave her to raise her young'uns.

I'd also leave the real old females since any female over eight feet is likely buttoned. And female gators don't usually get over eight feet. I'd just come back the next year and kill some shorts or something. The gators north of the Tamiami Trail, some of them just south of the trail, would button quicker than they did in the mangroves. Sometimes, even six-footers would button. Something in the water I guess. But down in the mangroves even the big ones didn't button. I've seen twelve-footers just as soft and pliable. That was the only thing good going for them, 'cause those gators were just about on starvation in them mangroves.

*   *   *

Damaged hides, any hide you could see light through when held toward the sun or light, brought two-thirds until about 1939. In the late 1930s, in the spring of the year, Argyle Hendry was camped on the north shore of Seven Palm Lake. Daily he would walk and hunt gators. After some two weeks, he stacked his rolled up hides at the foot of a cabbage palm and covered them with fronds. He walked into the swamp and when he returned he found that his cooking fire had crept under the hides. All his hides were really damaged—to about half their value. As he was nearly eighty at the time, he brought these hides and sad story to me. He had about twenty-five hides, and I bought them from him. This often happened—if there's a lot of dry stuff around and you're not plumb sure the fire's out, it will start creeping. No doubt camps have been burned out this way.

If light could be seen through the hide when you held them up toward the sun or the moon then the hides were considered damaged and a third of the value was taken off. This no doubt had an effect on the way a gator was skinned. Buck Rohrer skinned the best of any man I know of. The Indians also did a good job. On a few times I called some hides "damaged" that ordinarily would have got by as good. When you grow up in a place where people haven't treated you very good, more'n apt you would learn to treat people kinda like they treated you. I realized this when I was thirteen and worked for a dollar a day planting tomatoes—only to not get paid. Once Ed Brooker offered me a dollar to skin a large nurse shark in 1928; eight years later I got paid by "damaging" some gator hides that he was selling me [saying the hides were damaged, then paying Ed Brooker less for the hides than their market value]. Another time in the early 1930s a fellow who was down on his heels, young'uns starving, sold me a Model T Ford for five dollars. He said he'd have the title the next day. On the next day when I was supposed to pick up the car, I found out that he had sold it again; the car and he were gone. Well by and by he brought me some gator hides. He allowed they belonged to his dad and asked me to treat the old man right. By "damaging" enough to get my five dollars back, the debt was settled.

Buying Hides

For a while, there weren't many hide buyers here. In the early '30s, you could sell some at Bert Lasher's Indian Village on the Miami River—but this was off and on.[14] Fellas would want to borrow some money or something, and I started buying hides from them. I'd make only ten cents a hide on average. I never made much off these hides. As the word got out, more and more people would bring me hides. Then I'd call around and try to get the best price for them. Some big buyers would then come down here and pick them up. Most of the time, to get the best price, you had to carry them somewhere—around Okeechobee or along the Tamiami Trail, even Kenansville and Tarpon Springs.

Before 1939, you could be open about hunting gators in Dade County. But, I never was—had to discourage the competition. Monroe County stayed open until just about when the park came in. In the early days, lots of hides were being sent from Miami to Louisiana. The big hide buyers from North Florida would come down here and then take the hides over to Louisiana. There were three big buyers in the state during the 1930s and 1940s: Fishhook Carter, Casper from St. Augustine, and the tannery in Tarpon Springs. Also many small pin-hookers.

We knew of only one hide buyer from around here that had any honor at all—and he had plenty. He was born about 1890 and named after President William McKinley. William McKinley Osceola, a full-blooded Seminole Indian, lived at Bert Lasher's until he moved to the Tamiami Trail in 1933 or 1934—then he began to buy hides. He would buy hides from both Indians and whites. He had a place on the south side of the Tamiami Trail about ten miles out from Krome Avenue. When we used to go there, the Indian kids would call Ed Brooker "Holiwogus" (meaning "no-good"), then laugh and run away. Will-

William McKinley Osceola, 1940.

iam McKinley Osceola was an important Indian in the tribe and was a good friend until he died. He bought gator and otters for many years and would treat you right. He always invited me to the snake dances. After he quit buying, he sold a few to me.

In 1941—right before the worst time of my life, which was being shanghaied into the army right after the lowdown bombing of Pearl Harbor—I had accumulated two fifty-five-gallon oak barrels of gator hides. The best price I could get was from a man named Casper in St. Augustine. We were writing back and forth. He wanted me to ship them by train, which I agreed to—if he would send the money in advance. He agreed but said that if the measurements and grades were not as they should be, according to him, I must make up the difference. He told me to label them as cowhides because Dade County was closed to gators. I bought a couple of cowhides from an acquaintance who was doing some butchering. Casper was buying cowhides too, so he was charged for them. When the money came, I put the cowhides over the gator hides and tied tow-sacking over the barrels. I took them to the F.E.C. platform. My heart was doing double-time, and my puckering string was activated—especially when the agent asked me where I got so many cowhides. I replied, "Well sir, it don't take many to fill a barrel, and there's a slaughtering pen west of Homestead." This went without a hitch.

There used to be a hide buyer named Carter who bought hides from a place a mile or so north of Canal Point on Lake Okeechobee. Carter was called "Fishhook" as he claimed to have sold a train boxcar load of fishhooks. Carter said he advertised those fishhooks all over the state and sold them by the thousands. He lived around Orange Lake but would come down to Canal Point periodically to buy hides. He'd let you know when he was coming and what he wanted. There would usually be a small crowd waiting for him to buy their hides at his Canal Point location, which sat on the ridge of the lake. It was a beautiful area, a great sand ridge full of pretty cypress trees.

Indian men and women would get there the night before and sleep on his front porch—waiting for him. There were a few other white people who sold to Carter, but they generally didn't have very much. That country was pretty well hunted down at that time. Carter's measuring table was around the back of the house. After measuring the length of a hide, we'd roll it back up and leave it beside the mark on the board—which marked its length. Another fella usually would write down the number and lengths of your hides. Carter always would pay in cash. As soon as Carter was through buying all those hides, he'd get drunk.

Glen with Fishhook Carter, a hide buyer, on Canal Point, 1939.

Sometime in the early 1930s, Ed Brooker and I took some hides to Fishhook's on Canal Point to sell. We left Homestead early and got to Carter's place about noon. We then went up a few more miles, and Ed visited his brother Henry, who lived on the ridge in a sumptuous home. We then went back down south to Belle Glade, and Ed talked to people he'd known years ago when rambling this country. Someone told us the best way to go home was take the road to La Belle then go south to the Tamiami Trail. As the day was spent, we pulled off the road, made a gator-nest bed, and spent the night. This was my first trip up here, and I was enjoying it. From La Belle to Immokalee, it was a rocky road. Ed got more whiskey in Immokalee and must have burned up about all his money by the time he got home. From Immokalee to the Tamiami Trail, the road was paved. We were in no hurry and spent another night as Ed wanted to stop along and talk to the Indians, some he'd known from the turn of the century. We stopped in every camp along the Tamiami Trail. These folks had really fallen on hard times; the old ones were the worst off. They said, "White men kill everything, nothing left for us, we starve." The Depression had hit them hard, the good times of the '20s were no more, and every camp was in bad shape except Bill Osceola's. He and his family were better off as he was a buyer and seller of fur and gator hides. Later after visiting the camps I wrote "The Declaration of Indian Penance":

Indian declare!
White man hyar!
I go whar?
White man yell!
Go to hell
Indian tell
Very well
If you swear
No white man there.

Live Gators, Crocs, and Snakes

I would try to sell anything I could—although there wasn't always a market for them—including rattlesnakes, crocodiles, and gator eggs.

Glen inspecting an alligator nest in a sawgrass marsh four miles east of Card Sound Road, 1939. Eggs were sold for ten cents each.

The Piper Brothers, in Bonita Springs, always bought live crocodiles (live gators weren't worth very much). The Piper Brothers had an attraction in Bonita Springs—some kind of reptile garden along the Imperial River.[15] In the 1930s, live crocodiles that were over six feet long sold for twenty-five or thirty-five dollars. I never sold many large alligators, although I could get fifty cents for them babies. You used to see people set up along the roads selling baby gators for a dollar each.

Argyle Hendry was best known for catching crocs and selling them to wildlife shows around the country—especially to the Piper Brothers. He became very possessive of the crocs in Florida Bay and would tell you firmly that they belonged to him. "You can have the gators, but leave the GD crocodiles alone," he told me. Once when I came into Argyle's camp, there was a gallon paint bucket full of coffee steaming on a black mangrove fire. He offered me a cup of coffee. When I poured some liquid into the cup, I noticed the bucket was filled with coffee grounds and dead mosquitoes; there was no room for a full cup of coffee. He was quick to tell me that he just kept adding grounds to the

Glen, in 1996, holding the remains of a 1930s crocodile pen that was used to ship live crocodiles on the Florida East Coast Railway.

bucket and that "it wasn't over a week old." I acted like I was sipping it until he turned his head, then I poured it out. Anyway, I think he would have as soon killed you as let you have any of his crocs.

Mr. Hendry was camping on Manatee Creek in a 12' x 12' tin shack. This was his last camp, and he stayed there from 1942 until about 1960 when he died. Old man Hendry would keep his crocs, with their tails tied around close to their bodies, in a skiff in the shade of the mangroves—if he knew they were going to be picked up soon. Other times, he would tie them by their snouts and keep them overboard in the water. This is dangerous though since they can sometimes drown this way.

In the early days of the railroad, the crocs were shipped by train. I saw one such a-holding pen, that I first came across in 1936, in the mangroves along the railroad just this year. There was another pen in the middle of Joe Bay, which was probably used by Alligator Joe who later had a tourist trap showplace in Miami. If man had never caught or killed a crocodile, it's doubtful that they would be any thicker than they are now. Maybe there would be a few more big ones, but few babies can make it today in Florida Bay and its creeks. The reason why? The sea is rising; the old nesting spots up the creeks now stay too wet. Today the crocs seem to nest on the sand spits, and few, if any, can survive the long trip back up the creeks. My mother, who lived for upward of a year in a palmetto house at Madeira Hammock in 1893, said that her mother kept the kids back from the water and always had a gun at hand because of the crocodiles.

Casper from St. Augustine used to buy a lot of live gators and crocs from me during the 1940s. Generally, he would come down to Homestead and get whatever I had for him. On one occasion, in 1944, he sent a fella who wasn't from around here to pick up the animals. This Yankee wasn't used to live snakes and crocs. That fella came to my house on the Long Glade in a sedan that had a trunk in the back. We piled his car with snakes tied in sacks and put a tied-up, nine-foot crocodile into his back seat. I also had a number of young gators (three- and four-footers), along with some hides, that we put in his trunk. Even the word "crocodile" made that boy uneasy—don't think he ever made a trip our way again for Casper.

During the Depression years I tried to get permission from the State of Florida to open a gator farm—in 1939. For years, I had saved a bunch of gators in a pen that was behind the house where my mother was living on Krome Avenue [in Homestead]. Every time I went into the woods, I would bring some baby gators out with me and then raise them. Instead of giving me permission to start a farm, the state sent a warden to arrest me. The game warden gave me a week to turn the gators loose. I took them to Bonita Springs and sold the three hundred three- and four-footers for thirty-five cents each to the Piper Brothers. It took two trips in a Model A Ford to get them all there.

Dodging for Common Sense and Safety

Bringing hides home got to be a problem after Dade County frowned on their possession in or about 1939. Monroe County was open until or about the time of the park's takeover in 1947. If we was working out of the lakes, creeks, ponds, and marshes in Monroe County, we was alright until we come into Dade. So for a long time we traveled at night and got by. Moonshining had about stopped by then off from the old Ingraham Highway, so we weren't bothered by the prohis. But, before that, early in the '30s, the prohis stopped me often and would give me a going-over looking for a little sign that might connect me with moonshine. One time a prohi and a game warden walked into my camp—somebody had to have told them where it was—and the warden tried to give me a hard time. The prohi said, "Aw, leave that boy alone." And they left. I moved the camp.

Every few years if the water was down in the spring, I'd be dropped off where the Gum Slough is cut in two by the Loop Road to ramble the old gator holes to the south.[16] About three miles south of the Loop Road the slough forks—one strand goes westerly and the other easterly. Both strands were well represented with gator homes. On one trip of a week's ramble, my ride was supposed to find me on the Loop Road west of the Chicken Farm—wherever I came out. I stayed on the swamp side of the canal where the bushes was so thick you could only see a vehicle when it got opposite you. I'd brought a little flashlight to signal with. Not long after dark, I heard something coming on the rock road. Just as the car came by, I recognized it and shined the light. My ride made a hand signal that meant no and kept going. A few hundred yards behind him was a deputy sheriff. His car was recognizable. Umm ba ha, more trouble. I had heard that this sheriff was against anyone gator hunting but himself, and I was worried about my ride if he stopped him. After crossing the shallow canal on some limbs, I hid the hides and waited and worried. After a while the deputy must have stopped at someone's house. My ride went on a ways seeing no one behind; he then came back. We loaded in a hurry and got going. I was nervous as a flea on a greasy sideburn going that forty-five miles to home; I bet the seat was hardly touched. We'd made it again.

When on long walking trips of several days, I toted everything in tow sacks, fertilizer sacks—as in them days many things come in tow sacks. Nowadays people use a backpack, strapped on their backs. It is a wonderment to me as to how you get rid of a backpack in a hurry if you slip or trip and fall. I've fallen a jillion times, dropping my load as I fell. There were times that I'd fall on purpose.

Before bulldozers the pines that bordered the glades west of Loveland Road hadn't been cleared; a winding log road went through the woods to the edge of the glades. I was to meet my ride at the road at dark. When I got close, the woods were smoking, a sign that someone had set a fire while I was gone. Keeping clumps of bushes between me and the end of the road, I tried to stay hid as much as possible. Many narrow scrapes teaches you that you can't be too cautious. At dusky dark, I saw a man about one hundred feet ahead. There were many small rock holes along this margin, and so I acted as though I had fallen into one of these. When I was getting out I kicked my rolled-up sack of gator hides under a rock ledge. Acting a little crippled, I came up to the warden and asked him why they was burning the woods. He asked me if I'd had any luck, as they always do. The next morning at daylight I went back there and got what I'd hid.

For sixty years we walked and glade skiffed these glades. In the earlier years we never met anyone except a few Indians—and not many of them. There was very little concern about getting interrupted by law officers until the blowflies began to fly in the late 1930s. By the mid-1940s, there must have been fifteen of those blowflies being used to hunt the glades. There were also three landing strips in the glades west of town; two were near my camp on Pine Island. The runways were short, and they would only use them during the day.

We were uneasy about them and learned to hide from them if possible. I often would carry a bushy brush top with me to hide under when they was flying. Eugene Saunders, who often deer hunted nearby, said if he seen a hammock moving—he knew it was me. The blowfly boys could do as they pleased, and they always knew where the law was. No doubt, they told the game wardens about us, as we were stopped more often after we started seeing those planes.

During the late '40s gator carcasses were being thrown out close to my home and not by me. We took most carcasses miles from home and put them in some thick bushes. The game wardens no doubt figured the close-by ones were mine, and they were hot after me. In 1947, one of two wardens approached me and said he knew what I was doing and said he would like to go in cahoots with me. He said that he would tell me when he saw a gator on his rounds and that he'd let me know when he was in another direction. He told me that he realized how I kept things to myself and could be trusted. He could use a few extra dollars. I told him he was barking up the wrong tree. Anyway this didn't set too well with me, and since the park had also just come, we made plans to slip away at night. We moved to Okeechobee to hunt there for awhile since I knew people there that were frog and gator hunting. Those two wardens were old poachers that had got to be wardens. They knew everyone here.

*   *   *

After moving to Okeechobee in the fall of 1947, I got a job working for the government dipping cows and trying to kill out the Texas fever ticks. These ticks were threatening the cattle business in Florida.[17] The government had built large vats where the ranchers would have to bring their cows every two weeks to get dipped. Generally, the big ranchers had their own vats. The vats held a combination of DDT and arsenic. There was several dipping crews of five or six men, counting the boss, that went to a different vat everyday within about forty miles of Okeechobee City. I had a friend who lost his pocketknife in a vat, and he dove in after it. This being an arsenic vat, the poor devil broke out in large sores and nearly died. The crew had to force the cows down a shoot that made them jump into the vat. After swimming across the vat, the cow would jump out into a corral. Once they were in the corral, a couple of men would lean over its high rails and pick the ticks off the cows. The cows usually were real angry, and you had to lean way over the rail, hanging on with one leg, when trying to get to the ticks on the cows. The foreman could tell that I was downright terrified of the cows, so he gave me a paintbrush to mark the cows that had already been dipped.

But, like everything else, I was not good at it and only fooled the bosses for a few months. The government paid us ten dollars a day to dip cows in the daytime, and while we was at it we learned where the ponds and creeks were and how best to get to them at night. When we got off, Clifford Quarles, Bob Joiner, and I would hunt frogs and gators—they were paying off better anyway.

We would hunt the Allapattah Flats area around Okeechobee. There was a road of sand through the Bluefield Farms, and it went into the Allapattah Flats; some of this area was being farmed in 1947.[18] In days agone the flats were probably a large half-mile wide river somewhat like the Everglades—beautiful. Clifford Quarles and myself had walked for two days in the flats and had accumulated two tow sacks of hides and a hell of a thirst. This thirst brought on some carelessness, and that can be disastrous. About sundown, after not seeing anyone, we come on the road and put the sacks against a cabbage palm. Since we didn't see any sign of anyone we took a melon from an old watermelon patch. We busted one and began to eat and walk further into the patch looking for a better one, when we heard a vehicle. Oh, my God! A jeep with two wardens in it pulled up right by our sacks of hides. I whispered to him, "Remember Red, them hides ain't ours." (Clifford was redheaded.) My heart felt as big as a watermelon that was trying to beat its way out of my chest. They had to see the bumpy looking sacks. I knew we had at least lost two days of hard work. All of a sudden they turned around and left. They must have surely thought we had watermelons in the sacks. Our ride came soon after that, and we lucked out again. Pure, unadulterated luck.

No common sense was used that night. Had I been alone, those sacks would never have been left in plain sight, and the watermelon eating would have went on in a hiding place. When two or more fellows are together they tend to get careless. It was well known that Bluefields was a well-protected place for wildlife. As a side note, the Allapattah Flats was to me as beautiful a region as any in the world, although I had only seen pictures of the rest of the world.

We had been camped in an old house about eleven miles southeast from a town near the Upthegrove Grade on the rim of the big Lake Okeechobee. The water was sure enough high, so a boat was used to get from the road to the house. The gators and frogs were everywhere, and the price was good. Frog legs brought sixty-five cents a pound, and gator hides were a dollar a foot for flatskins six feet and up. Even three-footers brought a dollar a piece.

In the spring of 1948, me and Red Quarles drove a Model A Ford into a creek strand some three miles off the Indian Town Road and killed a few gators. We came back to the Model A and noticed some large tire tracks. We discussed who might belong to the tracks. Red said not to worry as he recognized the tracks as the ranch foreman's. He said he knew the man, and that we'd have no trouble. Umm ba ha! Well now the foreman thought that our truck belonged to a well-known turkey hunter that they'd been trying to catch. So when we stopped at the cattle gate that let you get on the hardtop highway to town, two game wardens jumped up from the palmettos (one on either side of the truck with drawn revolvers). It didn't take long for them to find the gator hides behind the seat. They told Red to drive to the courthouse, and they would follow.

About a mile up the road, the wardens motioned for Red to pull over. When he stopped, they told him to come over to their jeep. He was told that if he would divulge the name of his hide buyer, they would turn him loose. Umm ba ha! Him not thinking quick enough, he answered "What kind of a sorry ———— do you think I am?" That got him a court session and a six-month suspended sentence. But he did tell them that I was not hunting with him, and that he was just giving me a ride to town. This got me off. If he had only told them that he didn't know where he could sell the hides, he probably would have been turned loose.

The wardens did say they wanted to look around our houses. I was put off in town, and a friend I knew drove to my house and moved everything away and hid it. There was over a hundred skins hanging on the fence back of the house, covered with corn sacks. He quickly moved them. I went to some kinfolks' house and stayed until after dark, as I was afraid of being followed. As far as is known, my diggens was not searched. I was only hunting with and buying from a small bunch of fellows that could be trusted. But I knew it was about time to move camp.

* * *

Mike Tsalickis was a teenage Greek lad and was in the live snake business. He also started a roadside zoo in Tarpon Springs, a showplace for travelers. He was hooked up with a Greek-run tannery in Tarpon Springs, which I also did business with as they gave me a better price for hides than the local buyers. The tannery was looking for a man to work at buying gator hides in the south end of the state, and young Mike took this on. By continuing to catch snakes and buying gator hides, he was doing good.

However, there was others doing the same thing, especially in the gators, and they didn't want their business to be cut in on. So he began to be stopped often as word was getting to the wrong people. He was too open and would buy hides from anybody, which is a good way to get yourself caught. The tannery told him to look me up, and we did some dealings. He was a nice young man; we would hunt together.

He taught me how to catch snakes. To catch a nonpoisonous snake, he would grab it by the tail, swing it between his legs, close his legs, and the head would be trapped behind him whipping about. He then would slide one hand down the snake and then catch the snake's head when he got to the end. This method kept you from getting chewed up. This was done very fast. He could catch many snakes in a short period from the glade skiff at night using a headlight.

In 1948, I was supposed to meet Mike Tsalickis on the west side of Clewiston after dark to sell him some hides. After passing a certain filling station in town, Mike was to take in behind me. Then when we got to the pulling-off place, Mike was supposed to pass me and drive behind some bushes. He followed me for a mile or so out of town, when I noticed a vehicle without its lights on about a quarter mile behind us. Mike passed me and motioned me to pull over. I had no way of telling him about the car without lights. I just kept on going at about 35 miles per hour. He dropped behind me again and waved for me to pull over. I kept the same speed.

At that point, two game wardens in a jeep, now with their lights on, pulled him over. I kept the same speed. One warden got out and stayed

Glen leaning against a truck with a false-bottom bed, 1948. Alligator hides were kept hidden in a concealed box under truck bed.

with Mike. The jeep continued on and pulled me over. On the back of the homemade truck was a number three washtub. He grabbed that the first thing. It had a few cabbage [palm] leaves in it. When I questioned him as to what this was all about, he explained that they had just pulled over a hide buyer and thought I was with him. I was shook up. He was apologetic. This was a nervous night for me.

When we cut down this Model A, making it into a truck, we put a box (3' x 3 1/2' x 10" deep) with a sliding top that was used for the truck bed. We put the spare tire behind the box to hide it. Nobody outside the business was told about this box. That night, when I was pulled over, the box was full of around one hundred hides, which represented several weeks of work. For years this box was used when necessary. That night this box was worth it all, and it saved us many times. After finishing with the wardens, I went into La Belle and stopped for awhile for a cup of coffee. Then I went back to our camp on the Hillsborough Canal, near the Brooker Lakes. After a few years, Mike quit the glades trips and begin spreading out in Spanish country. He was headquartered in Laticia, Colombia, on the Amazon. I visited him there in 1954.

Flamingo and the Cape

C H A P T E R   4

The town of Flamingo, lying on the eastern edge of the Cape Sable Prairie, existed as an isolated fishing village for approximately sixty-five years prior to the establishment of the national park. From the late 1920s to the 1930s, Glen Simmons often camped along the shore at Flamingo, using it as a base camp before hunting the cape's lakes, ponds, creeks, and the backcountry waterways beyond Whitewater Bay. Later, in the 1940s, Glen lived with his wife in a number of small stilt houses at Flamingo on a more permanent basis. Glen's relationship to the area dates much further back though; his grandfather Duncan C. Brady is credited with giving Flamingo its name in 1893 (Tebeau 1963, 106). Although it remains an important launching site into Florida and Whitewater Bays for Everglades visitors, today's Flamingo bears little resemblance to the transitory outpost it once was. Both the completion of the Ingraham Highway, with its associated canals and drainage ditches, and the infamous Labor Day

Hurricane of 1935 dramatically contributed to the area's environmental and cultural evolution.

The "Cape," as it is called, is really composed of three capes that jut into the warm, shallow waters of Florida Bay. Just behind the sandy beaches of East and Middle Capes lies Lake Ingraham; long and narrow, Lake Ingraham was formerly called Long Lake or Whitewater Lake by the early settlers who fished and hunted its once-fresher waters. To the west, Little Sable Creek connects Lake Ingraham to Northwest Cape and Florida Bay. North of Lake Ingraham and extending eastward to Flamingo lies the Cape Sable Prairie. Before the construction of canals into the prairie, W. S. Blatchley described the area saying, "The soil, or rather the surface, is a grayish marl . . . and, except along the brackish inlets and sloughs, supports only a prairie-like vegetation of weeds and grasses" (1932, 277–78).

The northern boundary of the prairie is ringed with mangrove; a number of lakes then punctuate this dense mangrove country. Of these lakes, Glen primarily camped and hunted around the more inland, and remote, Cattail and Fox Lakes. Continuing on, the watery landscape of mangrove and glades—north of the Cape Sable Prairie—merges into Whitewater Bay. Edward Reimann aptly describes traveling through the Whitewater Bay complex as an almost surreal experience, noting, "Looking across the bay one can see what appears to be the opposite shore, but strangely enough, on reaching this supposed shore, he finds only islands, with the opposite shore still eluding him by appearing to be in the original position" (1940, 77). Even as late as 1940, only a few "hunters, trappers, Seminole Indians, and possibly a few people whom they have guided through" could negotiate these inland waterways (Stimson 1940, 80). Moreover, the gladesmen navigated the bay and backcountry rivers, which snake north and northeast of Whitewater Bay, without the help of charts or maps.

Until the years during World War II, Flamingo's population remained small, primarily composed of a few core families of fishermen. Like frontier communities throughout the country, Flamingo attracted a breed of men who sought the freedom of this isolation. The locals used to say, "The insane people went to Chattahoochee [site of the Florida State

Hospital for the Insane], but the real bad ones went to Flamingo." If not the "real bad ones," then at least the stridently self-sufficient remained at Flamingo. Drinking water had to be collected off rooftops; the summers were hot, humid, and buggy; and the village offered little protection from tropical storms. In 1919, Blatchley describes his journey across the Cape Sable Prairie from the Model Land Company's club house, three miles east of East Cape, saying, "This morning a Dr. King . . . and I took the one mule-wagon, the only vehicle kept here, and drove across the prairie, eight miles eastward, to Flamingo, the solitary settlement on the coast between here and Homestead. A number of deserted houses were passed along the way which had been abandoned by settlers who had grown tired of the isolation, the ever present hordes of mosquitoes and occasional hurricanes" (1932, 283).

Yet the fishermen, hunters, and the families who lived at Flamingo seemed to project an almost unyielding stoicism in the face of these difficulties. For instance, Glen recalls a conversation that he and Dr. Charleton Tebeau had with Louis Loudon, a long-time Flamingo resident. According to Glen, when Tebeau asked Loudon why he put up with Flamingo's inhospitable conditions for more than forty years, Loudon replied, "I thought that as much would overtake a man as he could over take." Strikingly, Glen's narrative reveals not only the difficulties of the backcountry settlement but also the profound sense of community shared by those living at Flamingo. Glen's recollections resonate with these images of community: men dancing around campfires on the moonlit Cape Sable Prairie, or families seeking shelter from a hurricane together in the Coot Bay Hammock.

After the early 1920s, with the completion of the Ingraham Highway (also called the Cape Sable Road and the Homestead Canal), Flamingo became directly linked to Homestead for the first time. Prior to the completion of the road, all supplies and visitors were delivered into Flamingo on freighters, schooners, and fishing and coal boats. But this road-drainage effort was actually only partially successful. Although it became possible to drive from Homestead to Flamingo, road conditions were at best unpredictable and usually untenable during the rainy season. The mud was so deep for the last five miles of the Ingraham Highway that trucks and cars would literary bog down to a complete stop (Glen half jokes when he says, "Yeah, you could use the road, but it was pretty hard on those pushing.") The Ingraham Highway–Homestead Canal, along with other smaller drainage efforts, also did little to open up the Cape to farming, as was intended. In fact, instead of draining the Cape Sable Prairie, these canals may have only "salted up the marsh," as Glen suggests. Yet for the gladesman, these road and inland waterways became essential routes to the region's backcountry lakes, ponds, and glades, making these destinations immediately more accessible.

The Labor Day Hurricane of 1935, the worst storm to hit the mainland of Florida, was arguably the second pivotal event in the history of the pre-park Flamingo–Cape Sable region. As the eye of this storm passed over nearby Matecumbe Key, it ripped out forty-two miles of filled railway bed and left behind only scant traces of the communities that lay in its path. Of the thousand or so people living in the area, approximately four hundred lost their lives, including hundreds of former World War I veterans who died when their rescue train, all but the locomotive, was swept into the sea (Parks 1968). While casualties were comparatively minimal at Flamingo, the hurricane completely destroyed all the permanent structures there, sparing no one from the tragedy of the storm. A month after the hurricane, Alexander Sprunt Jr., assistant director of the Audubon Sanctuary, flew over Cape Sable. His field notes reveal the dramatic impact of the storm:

> We went on then to Flamingo, or rather to where Flamingo had been. Not a stick or a stone remains of it. A tottering line of piles projecting into the Bay told me where the four houses had been, but had it not been for those piles and the chart in front of me I would never have known that I was within a hundred miles of Flamingo. . . . At Middle Cape, where we had dropped a bag of mail in April to the owner of the coconut grove there, we circled and looked for remains of his house. We could not even be sure of where the house had been. The grove was absolutely gone, only scattered palmettos . . . stood. It was a wonderful illustration of the Biblical term of "abomination of desolation."

A stand of dead black mangroves on East Cape Sable a few years after the 1935 hurricane. Courtesy Alexander Sprunt IV.

By 1939, Flamingo's size had dwindled to only twenty-one residents who lived in six stilt houses—that compared to a prehurricane community of twenty-five houses (Federal Writers' Project of the WPA for the State of Florida 1939, 236).

The ecological damage caused by the hurricane was also immense. The bird watcher Helen Cruickshank and her husband, Allan, a wildlife photographer, recall a trip taken down the East Cape Canal three years after this devastating storm:

> *In spite of the passage of years the canal was choked with hurricane wreckage. The country looked dead. Skeletons of mangroves were bleached white. Great mounds of debris lay in disorderly heaps. Streamers of pale marine grass, grayed and limp, hung high in the tops of the dead bushes and trees where it had lodged during that frightful storm. It looked like once gay confetti, pallid from long days in the sun, and that macabre thought made a shiver creep along my spine as I recalled the tales of horror told about that storm. . . . Now, years after the storm, no green showed itself and only the dead gray of twisted trees and barren, brown, muddy banks of the canal could be seen on either side. With the motor useless in the choked canal, we moved slowly. (1948, 76)*

The destruction caused to the ecology of the Cape was in some cases permanent. Most notable, an extensive forest of black mangrove that grew on the East Cape was destroyed. Daniel B. Beard, Everglades National Park's first superintendent, suggests in his 1938 report to the U.S. Department of the Interior that it was probably a combination of the hurricane and earlier drainage efforts that led to the decline of this famed stand of black mangrove (Beard 1938, 20). Importantly, Glen's account provides a rare glimpse into the cultural and ecological landscape of the Cape and Flamingo before and after the Labor Day Hurricane of 1935.

Living at Flamingo

Many people today have kinfolks that once made a living in and around South Florida after the Indians were mostly removed. Then they felt safe to live the backwoods life where they could make a living off the natural resources—such as cutting buttonwood, fishing, burning charcoal, hunting plume birds, gators, otters, coons, deer, and such. These people mostly lived in homemade palmetto and wooden shacks, eating salted mullet, birds, and turtles, doing anything that would make them a living. My mother's folks were no different. They raised eight healthy young'uns and lived on a dozen or more shores in the Keys and the Ten Thousand Islands from 1885 on—until the young'uns were of marrying age, and they scattered out. But some people stayed or were connected with the area until the park people eventually got them out.

In my time, Flamingo was a backwoods village of stilt houses. There was seldom over a dozen worthwhile homes, mostly shacks that were occupied by menfolks. The cotton-picking crew also would come to Flamingo and camp for a few months every winter (from the early 1930s until about 1970). This must have added about fifty to the population every winter. People used outhouses that hung over the water along the docks. Fresh water was always a problem there. People caught rain off their roofs and mostly stored it in tanks, drums, and a few

Flamingo in the late 1930s. Courtesy Alexander Sprunt IV.

Aerial photograph of Flamingo, 1947. The cotton-crew camp and dock (foreground); the white house and dock (center) belonged to Coleman Irwin; the third dock and house (from foreground) belonged to Kay Irwin.

cisterns of concrete. Water was used sparingly in the dry season. Groceries were either brought in by run boats or fish trucks. The fish companies that you worked for charged you for groceries and credited your account. There were no schools or stores when I was there. Sometimes the hurricanes almost cleaned the shore of all the houses. When this happened, lumber was scrounged for building back. Some people got lumber from the do-good organizations.

In the summer, the skeeters were always bad at Flamingo. They weren't as bad during the winter, but you wouldn't want to lay outside without a skeeter bar. I stayed with Louis Loudon on an old boat just off shore from Flamingo for a few weeks in May of 1934. I don't remember why I was staying with Louis, but we slept on that boat at night. But one night, when I was onboard, I heard an actual roar. When I heard it, I knew damn well that the skeeters were coming by the million. Well it wasn't a loud roar, but it got my attention. After a few minutes from hearing it, the skeeters was on me. At Flamingo, people had to build smokes out of black mangrove, and they kept them burning all the time outside of their houses during the summer. Yeah, people smelled like smoke. I used to use it all the time. Your old clothes would get kinda yellow looking. But, you know, nobody seemed to care. I love the smell of black mangrove smokes, I didn't mind it at all.

Some people had accommodations in town and spent time in both places. A lot of people came and went, stayed awhile, and then moved on. A few families owned land and built better homes there. Seldom did over fifty people live there in the 1930s. A few more lived there in the 1940s—as during the war years fish was in good demand. The Roberts and Irwins were always tied to Flamingo from about the turn of the century.[1] They had homes in Florida City and Homestead, and they came and went. The young going to in-town schools. The kin of these folks always were welcome, so it seemed. Mrs. Loren Roberts set a good table, and everybody was invited to eat.

Flamingo was more than a fishing village in the earlier days after the Indian removal and the Civil War. A lot of buttonwood [a very hard wood] and boat timber was cut from the surroundings. They grew sugarcane and made syrup there, burnt charcoal, and smuggled whiskey. You can still see the signs of the kilns. In the early 1890s, my Grandpa Brady made a good living thereabouts, cutting buttonwood for charcoal off the Cape and shores of the Ten Thousand Islands.[2] Later he had to move to Sand Fly Pass and Chokoloskee so his kids could get schooling. But he still kept up a freight route to Key West hauling wood, charcoal, and farm produce.

There were two big prairies on Cape Sable, the Raulerson Prairie and the Flamingo Prairie. The Flamingo Prairie [also called Roberts Prairie] was kind of a marl and soup-doodle prairie, sometimes very wet. But there was some humps in it where things had started growing up on an old gator nest or something. There were some trees all through the prairie. You could drive across the prairie from Flamingo to the East Cape Canal—the cotton crew had built a road there—just a little bit above the glade plane. You could drive on that, but occasionally you'd get stuck. If it was real dry, you could drive all over that Flamingo Prairie.[3]

Duncan C. Brady (right), Glen's grandfather, on his schooner at Key West, circa 1890.

If some rain came, these boys from Homestead would go down there just to play with their cars. When the prairie got wet, it was just as slick as glass. Those boys would drive just as fast as they could, then turn the wheel a little and away she'd go—'round and 'round, a-sliding in the mud. The cars would spin around there four or five times. Scary as the devil. But I don't think they ever turned one over. They had certain places on the prairie where they could do it, if there wasn't any growth. They'd take their old daddy's car down into that salty mud on Sunday, and he wouldn't know about it. Many automobiles were ruined that way.

During the winter nights, the men who lived at Flamingo would sometimes come out to the prairie, gather up around buttonwood fires, roast some coots, and drink some moonshine. They'd have the fires not too far from the water, just in front of the houses—have a big ya-ya and have fun. One fellow had an old squeeze box, some of them would be dancing in the prairie. Buck-stomping. For fun they'd have some shooting parties out there. The men would gang up on sides, get in the trees, and shoot at one another. It's amazing that they didn't kill one another. They wouldn't shoot right at them, you know. They had a different way of having fun in them days.

On one cool winter night, in 1934, I remember some fellows were roasting coots and drinking some 'shine on the Flamingo Prairie and just having a hell of a good time. There were several buttonwood fires going. Everyone was happy. Coleman Irwin, a man of much respect, was in no hurry to eat his coot—being as he was very particular about getting it perfectly done. The coots were cooked on a stick, turning them often. I fixed a coot on a stick and started to roast it. Coleman and I were both using the same fire, so thinking I'll play a trick on him, I swapped my bloody coot for his cooked one when his back was turned. But I swear that I had no intention of eating his cooked one. I thought for sure as hell he'd notice it, and we'd laugh about it and change back. By God, he started eating that raw coot. The blood was running and squeezing out the corners of his mouth, and he was smiling. He eat that coot, and what was I to do? I eat his. But, for sure as long as he lived, no one else ever knew of it. The Irwins deserved much respect, my favorite people.

*　　*　　*

There is nothing better to eat than a Cape Sable coot. After a few weeks in the marshes west of Flamingo, they would get so fat and plentiful. Other places they tasted muddy; the guts are green. But anyone that ever lived down there can tell you, them coots around Flamingo had fat that was snow white and a quarter-inch thick. The guts were clean. God were they good. A few miles from Flamingo, Slagle and House put [drainage] ditches in there in the early 1920s that led into the Bay. The ditches were supposed to drain the marsh, but instead they just salted it up. The ditches never amounted to much commercially since that area was never good for farming. But during the winter months, these ditches were always full of coots, teal, other ducks, and pond birds.

Watson's Fish Camp (also called the Shark River Fish Camp) under construction, winter 1940. The planked road leading to this camp on Coot Bay was the Syrup Kettle Trail. Courtesy Alexander Sprunt IV.

The coots came there in the winter, ducks too. After the 1940s, it seemed like the coots were getting scarcer. They used to come to the southwest region by the millions. Early settlers sold their gizzards for a nickel a piece. We used to pickle them down in salt brine and carry them with us on trips. When winter came, you could hear the coots and ducks flying over at night as you lay under your skeeter bar. If the prairie was under water, they'd settle there. There would be plenty in the ponds and lakes in the marshes. The teals came early, about October. Then the coots came. Seems like the teals stayed a long time. You could eat teals all winter long. The coots are gone now as man once knew them, along with other migratory birds.

About that time [early 1940s], an Audubon warden was hanging out at the Coot Bay Pond at Watson's Fish Camp. Coots were in the bay by the thousands and ducks too; there were rafts as big as half the bay.[4] Duck hunters just had a picnic in that bay. The Audubon warden, Barney Parker, would run his boat through the rafts like he was chasing a poacher. When the birds got up good the duck hawks would do their job.[5] So many hawks and coots, many of the coots would fall back to the bay after being hit by the duck hawks—and Barney would pick up his next meal. That sure saved shotgun shells. When Everglades National Park took over in 1947, Barney got to be a ranger.

*   *   *

Before the Labor Day Hurricane of 1935, there was hundreds of gopher turtles on Cape Sable. The turtles lived along the shell beaches on the Cape, especially along East Cape. In 1929 or 1930, somebody gave Frank Irwin Jr. and myself the idea that we could sell them and make some money. Frank's uncles lived at Flamingo (Kay and Coleman Irwin). Coleman told us that he would take us to catch gophers if we could get to Flamingo. We drove from Homestead along the Ingraham Highway in an old Model T Ford. We were just kids, maybe thirteen or fourteen years old, but everyone drove at that age. From Flamingo, Coleman Irwin took us to the East Cape on his boat. His boat had a car's engine on it—lots of people did that then since it was cheaper.

The people who lived at Flamingo didn't really eat many gopher turtles. I think they eat mainly green turtles that they'd catch in their nets. They didn't throw any green turtles back, you can be sure. But we thought we could peddle those turtles to people we knew and sell them to the Indians. The Indians would buy them if you could catch enough.

We had high hopes but didn't have a bit of knowledge as to how to get them gophers. We'd run an iron rod down into those turtles' caves and try to feel for their old stiff shells. We soon found that digging the turtles out of their caves was too much work, so we tried to run them down when they was out feeding. We tried to catch them out, before they got back into their hole. We only got some of them—as most got in their caves before we could head them off. We wound up with about thirty or so gophers.

It didn't take us long to decide we wasn't going to make a fortune at gopher hunting at fifty cents each. Even when you could find a buyer, most people wanted to buy them on credit. In those days payment was seldom, if you ever were paid. The Labor Day Hurricane of 1935 seemed to have almost got rid of the gophers on the Cape. It sure wasn't me and the Irwins.

The Roberts house at Flamingo, late 1930s. Courtesy Alexander Sprunt IV.

About a year or so after the bad storm of 1935 that had cleaned Flamingo of all living abodes, some houses had been put back on the shore, and docks rebuilt. The Roberts and the Irwins just built back; they got some money, I understand, from the Red Cross and such. Loren Roberts had a nice new stilt house some eight feet off the ground, and most people that come down to Flamingo, which was few or less at times, were welcome. Everyone just piled up at Loren's house. His wife didn't seem to think nothing about feeding twenty-five people. They were hospitable people.

In 1936, I was staying with Loren when some boys, kinfolks, had come on a mullet launch from Card Sound and stopped for the night at Flamingo. Fellows just bedded down on the floor of the screened porch—getting out of the skeeters. These boys were on a clam hunt around the west coast; they had stopped at a washed-out Indian burial mound on Cape Sable and found some large human bones. They carried on about how big the bones were. Uncle Steve Roberts was there, he was about eighty years old, but there was so much ya-yaing and laughing going on that he went out on the dock in the skeeters to get some rest.

Next morning they were leaving after breakfast. On a wall a couple of hats were hanging—they were about the same except one was gator-hunting grimy, and the other was church-going quality. The pretty one wound up on Argyle Hendry's head as he was going down the long steps. Loren was bidding them good-bye, then he added, "Mr. Hendry, can't you tell that grimy hat of yours from that new one of mine?" Loren got his hat back, and everybody got a laugh, even "Hogeye" Hendry who apologized.

Kay Irwin's house was also a favorite spot for the Flamingoites. Ward Roberts had a laugh that should have been recorded—when on a spree he laughed a lot, and when he laughed everybody else did too. Ward was talking and laughing, telling about some of the Flamingoites having a several day drink-a-thon at Kay's stilt house in the early 1940s. They liked Kay's place because of his hospitality and clean house, however during these fun times not much cleaning went on. The house was in a mess. Kay owned a pig that wasn't getting much attention so it invited itself to the party. These houses were put on poles, the floor being eight to ten feet above the ground. The pig climbed the stairs and pushed open the door. He took one look at the messed-up inside and said uh! uh! and went back down the stairs.

*   *   *

Some things that went on at Flamingo are better forgotten, but Crazy Sam must be wrote about—at least one or two happenings. In about 1934, I was camping on the shore of Flamingo with a fellow named Ira Davis, trying to make a living sea-trout fishing. The owner of a fish company, by the name of Flemming, brought a young man down to Flamingo who was, what Oman Barber would call, "one-sided." If he wasn't crazy he sure was putting on an act and a good one at that. Mr. Flemming had made a deal with Louis Loudon to keep and look out for Sam for the sum of two dollars a day. Louis Loudon was one of the world's noblemen. He seemed to reason out everything he said and not to fall into the backwoods-language ways of the locals. 'Twas said he'd walked to Flamingo in 1908 as a young man after someone put him off at about Cape Sable. He stayed at Flamingo most of his active life until about the time the park came, and he settled with his new wife, Ossie, a mile or so west of Homestead in about 1950.

Mr. Flemming hired Louis to look out for Sam during the day and keep him on an old fishing boat at night. This old boat had a low cabin with two bunks and a disabled motor. Louis would take Sam ashore in the day and try to keep him out of trouble, but from the tales that he told me — this wasn't easy. The happenings that Louis told me are worth repeating. One night Sam decided to swim to Miami and jumped overboard. Well now there ain't much water on top of the mud at Flamingo. One fellow said about the water at Flamingo, "The bottom is close to the top." So according to Louis, Sam didn't get far. Another time during the night Sam told Louis that a hurricane was going to hit them, and they must go to shore. Louis tried to reason with him, "No hurricane was coming, Sam!" Sam kept it up about a hurricane until Louis persuaded him that they could pole the boat over to some nearby net racks, tie up, and they would be safe. This suited Sam. The tide was up so they poled to the net racks and tied up close. Now these net racks were off shore a hundred yards or more. Sam was satisfied and went to sleep. Everything was all right until their bunks began to fill up with water. Turns out they had tied up over a broken net rack stanchion. When the tide went down, so did the boat — with the stanchion through the boat.

On another occasion, Louis made a deal with Ira Davis to watch Sam. Ira didn't care much about fishing but Louis wanted to go trout fishing — so he said. He probably just wanted to get away from Sam. Louis made a deal with Ira to keep the boy for two dollars a day — since that's what he was getting. This just suited Ira 'cause he needed something to laugh at. Ira and Sam wound up at my camp that evening. I had a fire going and was fixing supper. The coffeepot was close to the fire. Sam was looking around, and Ira had one of them smart-look snickers on his face. It's been sixty years or more, so there's nothing I can remember of what was said, but what he done was unforgettable. Sam picked up the coffeepot, cleared his throat, spit into the pot, and set it back down. I grabbed the pot and threw it overboard. Ira was urged to walk Sam back to Louis Loudon and tell him to keep Sam away. He left with him. But Louis talked him into keeping Sam for one more day. That evening, when I was coming back to my camp, I saw Sam throwing my new Stetson hat in the air and beating it with a stick. That was too much. You feel sorry for someone that crazy, but this going-on had to stop. I visited Louis, and he kept Sam away after that. It was told later that Sam was walking down the road to Homestead when he was picked up and carried out of my life.

Fishing from Flamingo

When I was there, Flamingo was mainly a fishing village. When the fishing was good, people would tow their houseboats there from the west coast and stay. Sometimes three to five fish companies operated from there. Some used lay boats and run boats to collect the fish. Some men thereabouts might fish on dark nights and drink up on moonlight nights. For the most part, they were sober and hardworking. Whiskey and beer could get mighty scarce around there at times.

There was also some sports fishing being done around the area. Louis Watson started a charter boat business out of Coot Bay in the 1930s. He later put in a canal that joined Coot Bay and the [Coot Bay] pond. This connection let people get into Coot Bay from the road [Ingraham Highway]. From Coot Bay, Watson would take people out to the Shark River to catch jewfish and other fish.

While I was mostly hunting, I decided to try a little fishing, since the money was good. My wife and I were living on Flamingo in 1944 in a house that Loren Roberts built and owned just west of Bradley Key. This stilt house was pretty good-sized; it had a couple of bedrooms and a cistern. Loren invited us to use the house because I was going to fish for him. He wouldn't take any money for rent. He said he had never charged anyone rent for a house of his. He was an exceptionally fine man. He would always pick me up and give me a ride to town if he came along when I was walking toward town.

The cistern on the house Loren gave us hadn't been used lately and was in bad need of cleaning, and the pump needed work. (The concrete cistern was about 15' x 15' and held about two feet of water. We used it to hold yearling gators until it was time to meet a buyer from

Aerial photograph of Flamingo, 1947. Loren Roberts's fish house sits on the dock.

St. Augustine named Casper.) So instead we used a "de-headed" oil drum to catch water from the roof. Of course we hauled some water when it was necessary or when we were coming from town. One morning when I was going to the oil drum for water, I found a hoot owl in the drum. This barred owl was near drowned. Owls ain't much good in water. The owl was lifted out and dried off some, then we took it upstairs and put it in the open doorway to finish drying off. Walking past the owl in the doorway didn't seem to spook it too much as it stayed with us till sundown. Then it flew to a coconut palm; that night a little hooting went on. My wife being a little finicky wouldn't use the water from the drum. This owl brought me on a trip up the canal about ten miles to get a barrel of water.

I eventually fished for the House Fish Company. I fished from my glade skiff and used cane poles. The skiff had a Briggs and Stratton motor in it. On the way back to Flamingo, I could guide that boat with my feet—so I could use my hands to gut the fish. The skiff rode so low in the water that people on shore weren't able to see the boat. They said that it looked like I was walking on water. I did a lot of bailing.

An unidentified man pushes a glade skiff in Florida Bay, late 1930s. Courtesy Alexander Sprunt IV.

There were about three or four fish companies on shore at Flamingo; the companies used a lay boat, which was kept offshore near the channel to collect the fish. Most people thereabouts hooked up with a fish company. About mid–1940s, there was a family of Mills on Flamingo. The man went by the name of "Tater," he was a good-sized, heavy-built man. For whatever reason, Tater decided to haul his own fish. He probably hauled his own fish to make more money and also because some of the companies were not too reliable. To haul the fish, he used a 1933—or about—one-and-half-ton Chevrolet with a covered body. Now anyone not living at Flamingo before the park came probably wouldn't believe how bad that road could get. The last five miles of the Ingraham Highway was all slippery mud during the rainy season, full of deep ruts. A regular automobile couldn't make it, and if it did it wasn't worth it to the people who was pushing it.

Not only was the road bad, but people hardly used it. In 1943, people were still poor and didn't waste gas going to Flamingo from Homestead if they could get fish closer. On the weekends, only a few souls might venture toward Flamingo. If the road was dry they'd have no trouble, but during the week mostly only fish trucks traveled the road, and they could have trouble. We had a high-wheel Model A Ford skeeter that would generally get in and out. Once, when my wife and I were returning to Flamingo from Homestead we broke down a mile or so past the stone bridge [also called the "concrete bridge"]. The stone bridge was just a few miles past the halfway mark between Flamingo and Homestead. We decided to wait for someone to come by and hopefully get us a rotary button from town. While we waited, we walk-hunted the canal along the road. We were still hunting on the second night of being stranded when a fish truck came by going to town. We

The Ingraham Highway heading toward Flamingo, September 1940. Courtesy Alexander Sprunt IV.

knew them, and they promised to bring us a rotary button when they came back. After three nights of fighting skeeters, sure enough, true to his word, the man returned with the part. We had seen no other vehicle. Only moonshiners and gator hunters put up with this swamp in the summer time, and the 'shiners had to give up the business, or almost. It was a lonesome road in summer but livened up some to about ten cars a week in winter. Then it was thirty-five miles from Flamingo to town; now the new road is about fifty—the park put a fifteen-mile whip in the road.

During the mid–1940s, the road was so bad that in order to get the fish trucks in and out of Flamingo, the local fishermen held a road repair party. I was invited to this party. The fish trucks hauled rocks from along the rocky part of the road to the muddy part of the road, west of the Snake Bight road. We threw basketball-sized rocks under the tires of the trucks to keep it above the mud. Everyone pitched in. My memory don't keep track of the number of loads we hauled, but I do remember a dinner break. Loren Roberts made coffee in a four-gallon pick bucket. If I ain't mistaken, he dumped a pound of Maxwell House coffee in that bucket. One sip and I cut mine with about four parts of canal water.

Anyway, about halfway up this same mud road, Tater's truck became disabled. The truck became stuck there and just about blocked the road for anyone else. The mosquitoes and deer flies were some kind of thick. The truck carried a few thousand pounds of fish and, after the ice melted in a few days, the truck began to stink. It grew worse everyday.

Since my vehicle was the only thing that would go to town, it brought on some woe and was one reason I was glad to leave Flamingo. There was some fellows that liked a beer now and then, and whether I wanted to go to town or not, generally at night, I would take them for a few dollars. Now if the wind was from the east or west, you was gonna smell Tater's truck within a quarter mile of where it was. We had no windows or doors on our truck to keep that smell out. If the road was bad, it took quite a while to get out of the smell (and it was bad).

A familiar sight on the road to Fla-mingo, September 1940. Courtesy Alexander Sprunt IV.

After so much time the fish rotted down to a stinking mull. Tater scraped it out and started driving the truck again. This stinking machine was his everything truck. Yep, he did his shopping with it. Seems he always parked on the south end of Washington Avenue, next to the railroad, when he was in town [Homestead]. Before you seen it, you would know he was in town, provided that the wind was right or wrong. My wife had a better nose than me, and she was always the first to say, "Tater's in town."

Hunting from Flamingo and the Cape

I fished very little, as the swamps suited me better. Before the park came, we would drive to Bear Lake and hunt from our glade skiffs, mostly looking for gators and otters in the lakes and ponds that are northerly of Cape Sable. During the 1930s, I didn't live in a house at Flamingo but camped along the shore there. We would use the Cape Sable Canal as a route to reach Mud Lake, Bear Lake, Alligator Lake, and the Fox Lakes. To get into the Cattail Lakes you had to go through Lake Ingraham then up Little Sable Creek and into the Raulerson ditch. This was a hand-dug ditch, so I was told, that a small creek that came from Little Cattail Lake met with. From Whitewater Bay and Oyster Bay, we'd travel up the many rivers, such as the Shark River, North River, Joe River, and the East River, that led into the mangroves and glades.

About 1922 the Middle Cape Canal was dug from the lower end of Lake Ingraham to the Gulf. This part of the drainage plan played particular hell with the environment. When the Middle Cape Canal was

East Cape Canal, 1946. During the winter months, the cotton crews built a bridge on the exposed pilings across the canal.

The bridge over the creek, which connected Bear and Mud Lakes, late 1930s. The structure could be removed by the cotton-picking crews. Courtesy Alexander Sprunt IV.

first dug a man could jump across it. The narrow dredge boat that dug it was leaking, and so the canal was dug just wide enough to allow the boat to squeeze through—this kept the boat from sinking as it held the mud in the seams.[6] When Wes Mobley and I were in there in the early 1930s, my sixteen-foot glade skiff would hang up in places if it got turned sideways. The current was so swift in there that your boat could get away from you real easy and hang up in the bushes on each side. Now the canal is about three hundred feet wide and no doubt getting wider, and it has washed a lot of the beaches away. The tide roars into the east end of the lake and roars out of the Middle Cape Canal at the other end. This process then reverses itself every six hours, all the time tearing the lake to hell. Some day the Cape will wash away.

The East Cape end of the lake is one hell of an indescribable mess and has no resemblance to the lake that man saw before dredging.[7] My grandfather D. C. Brady lived and took care of the Coconut Grove in 1893 at Middle Cape when my mother was four years old. He told of the birds and gators there in the lake. He called it Long Lake and said that freshwater perch lived there. The first thing the government should have done was close the two canals from Lake Ingraham to the Gulf of Mexico; even now they should be closed as time already has proven the ill effects the canals are having. Likewise, the ditch into Little Cattail should be closed, if it ain't already.

The Fox and Cattail Lakes

Little West Lake, one of the Fox Lakes, always paid off better than the other two. Why? Because it wasn't hunted as much because you had to drag a small boat about a quarter mile or so to get there. It wasn't easy, but we always did it—'cause it paid off. These lakes were called the Fox Lakes because the gators were foxy in them—'twas said that they wouldn't hold fire long enough to get a shot at 'em. We only found this to be true when the light danced off the white, dead buttonwood and scared them.

On one trip, Buck Rohrer and I saw some water moving and thought it might be a small creek that connected the second Fox Lake to Little West Lake. This creek took a lot of cutting as it was so badly overgrown. It was no wider than our glade skiff and snake-crooked. We finally got to the lake and hunted the night. From then on we used the creek, but we never told anyone about it or noticed any sign that anyone else had used it.

We always camped to the right of the dividing creek between the first and second Fox Lakes. This seemed to be the best we could find, and there was plenty of wood there. Sometimes it was wet ground but handy. Every time we was there I'd carve the date on a board that I found there; no doubt by now it has rotted away. I'd give an eyetooth for that board if I had one. The last time I was there to hunt was in 1947 or not much later. After that, people started hunting in there with little floatplanes. The gators became very scarce, and it was common to see carcasses piled up around the Fox Lakes.

*   *   *

Just after Pearl Harbor, me and Ted Walker made a trip to the Cattail Lakes. The water in these lakes was a little brackish, but there were some small creeks that ran into them from the glades. In the winter these lakes were full of migratory birds: herons, ducks, every kind of wading birds, coots, even some big old geese in there. The birds only stayed in them as long as the conditions suited them. There were a good many cattails in them, but the lakes were open enough to hunt.

We decided to try to drive across the Raulerson Prairie from Flamingo and enter the Cattails from the Raulerson ditch, if we could. We came across from Flamingo on the old road that led to Lake Ingraham. The House and Slagle ditches had permanent bridges on them. They had to because there used to be some traffic on this road. At the time, there was a commercial fish camp on the East Cape Canal, which was a safer place for boats than outside in the open gulf. The camp had two tin shacks on the mud side of the canal and a few net racks. They fished for pompano from there during the winter.

When we got to the East Cape Canal, the bridge was out. At the time, the government's wild cotton crews had built a bridge across the canal. Then the canal was about fifteen feet wide. But when they were not using the bridge, they would remove the planks off the trestles. Maybe they did this to keep somebody from stealing them or to keep people out. Ted and I scrounged some planks from some old net racks and piled them up till they looked strong enough to hold a Model A. We took a chance on driving across. The next canal into the lake still had the driving planks in place. So we made it to the Raulerson drainage ditch that joined Little Sable Creek with Little Cattail Lake.

The next evening, we made it to Big Cattail Lake. This lake was about a quarter of a mile across and ragged around the edges. On the western shore of Big Cattail, there was some tree growth—mangrove and buttonwood. It was a good place for birds to roost. They would cause you a little stress when you were hunting. Sometimes the clamor of the birds could scare the gators. The reason we hunted Big Cattail was because it was so hard to get to. Even though there were gators in that lake, not many people hunted it (until years later when I saw evidence of people hunting with a floatplane). It was worth getting to because they'd always be some gators. If you went in there every three months, it'd pay you. Sometimes it would turn out pretty good.

In the late 1930s, we used to drag our boats with all our gear from Little Cattail to Big Cattail. We'd drag the skiffs for the quarter mile that separated the two lakes and then drag it back after a few nights of hunting. Tall switchgrass grew between the lakes in bunches that were six or seven feet tall. We had to pull the boats over this grass, and it would kind of lay down as you pulled the boats over. Once we got into Big Cattail, we camped on the eastern shore—right where we walked in. It was a wet camp, but we didn't want to walk around too much during the daytime. The gators sometimes would see you, and that would put them on edge. Then they'd be more foxy, so we thought. Later on, we drug a small skiff into Big Cattail and left it.

I sunk the skiff in the black, muddy water about forty feet from the shore of Big Cattail, so I wouldn't have to haul another boat in. As we hunted there about four or five times a year, it was much easier. About 1940, I went looking for that boat, and it wasn't there. We spent some time looking for it by wading and swimming around in the lake. We then went back and drug the other boat into Big Cattail Lake and really looked for the other one. It was gone. We figured some other gator hunters had found it and rehid it somewhere else. But lo and behold! Sometime after that, in 1943, I was driving past the Coot Bay Pond, and there on the bank was the little glade boat—some twenty miles and a lot of swamp from Big Cattail Lake. With a little investigation, we found out the boat had been brought out by Don Poppenhager, who was transporting some oil hunters on his equipment—glade buggies and such—said he had found the "abandoned" boat. When I told Don that the boat was used to make a little grits money and that I'd have to take it back to the lake, he said, "No you won't. It'll be back in a few days." He apologized, and, true to his word, took it back. Sure enough on the next trip to Big Cattail, it was there. Imagine a man that would take that boat back twenty miles through that aggravation. After a life of ill treatment by fellow men, Don Poppenhager stood out, worth writing about. He was not a common man.

When Ted and I were on our trip right after Pearl Harbor, the boat was there, but we noticed smoke behind us toward Little Cattail. It was as dry as the devil that year, and the grass really burned. At dark, the place was lit up like it was high noon. It had turned into one big fire by sundown. The air was full of fire, sparks, and smoke. We spent the night keeping from burning up, and the lake stayed lit up all night.

We knew that we couldn't hunt that night. The gators would have been scared to death.

We had heard a motorboat in Lake Ingraham that day and figured someone was trying to mess us up. I figure someone set the woods on fire at the Raulerson ditch because they wanted us out of there. They wanted it for themselves. You couldn't hardly keep the people from Flamingo from knowing what you were doing. They'd see your glade skiff on the back of your truck as you passed near there.

We hunted the next night and did a little good. We had figured on staying longer but had made the mistake of putting our drinking water in a five-gallon gasoline can thinking maybe it would last longer if it tasted of gasoline. Well it sure did last longer, you couldn't stand to drink it. But whoever set the fire did his job well. This fire was blamed on me and as the county was in such a fear of the Japanese at that time all kind of rumors were circulating among the locals. They said that the FBI was looking for me. Let me tell you that there was some hellish people hereabouts.

Camping on the Joe River

When I was sixteen [in 1932], after trying to get work in town, I loaded my glade skiff on my Model T and headed down the Ingraham Highway. At the Syrup Kettle Trail I headed over the Coot Bay Prairie to Coot Bay. You could drive your car along the Syrup Kettle Trail, although it was a muddy prairie road. Syrup was made in that country when they were building the railroad to Key West. When I was young, there used to be two or three big iron syrup kettles left at the Coot Bay Prairie. The Coot Bay Prairie ran for fifty acres west of the Coot Bay and was bordered by buttonwood on each side. This prairie had been cleared and planted in cane. 'Twas said that the brick furnaces used for making the syrup were later used for whiskey stills.

I met up with Wesley Mobley and "Uncle" Steve Roberts, who were camped down near Coot Bay. Steve Roberts must have been at least seventy-five years old at the time. I stayed with them a day or two. It was very enjoyable listening to them talk. Wes Mobley didn't seem to talk much about the Ashley Gang, he being a brother-in-law to John. [8]

Coot Bay Landing, at end of the Syrup Kettle Trail (on the southeastern corner of the bay), late 1930s. Courtesy Alexander Sprunt IV.

His son, Hanford, was also a big player in the Ashley Gang. I don't think that I ever asked him anything about his early days.

After camping together, Uncle Steve Roberts walked on back to Flamingo, and Wes Mobley and I left for the North River in an old mullet skiff that had a five horsepower, one-cylinder Gray Motor. Wes towed my glade skiff, which I was never without, behind his boat. We stayed on the North River for two weeks and killed a few gators and a deer.

After we left the North River, we went into the Bill Ashley Camp.[9] The Joe River Marsh was one of the richest wildlife marshes in the country. Everything was there except turkey and quail. The region was full of migratory coots and ducks as well as flintheads and curlews. So many birds. I've seen thousands of wood ibis, white ibis, and buzzards ride the currents a half mile above my head along the Joe River. They would circle straight up for about a half mile, all the while flapping and riding those currents. Then they would fold their wings back and dive straight to the ground—as if they were aiming for me. Then they would pull out ten feet over my head with a deafening roar. If you didn't know they were diving, it would buckle your knees.

Wes and I knocked around together for six months off and on, never making much money but living good. We were hunting gators, otters, coons, and doing some fishing in all the old lakes, gator holes, and rivers. Wes Mobley was quite a man in the swamps for his age—around sixty at the time, at least I figured so. I remember when he was surprised his eyebrows would go up to his hairline. When we needed supplies, he would send me into town. Wes Mobley always stayed in the backcountry.

When we were on this camping trip we were trying to stretch our fresh water out so we could stay longer. Every way we could, we'd use river water. During the dry spring of the year, the water could get near about like seawater. Well, rice was cooked with a lot of water till it was nearly done, then all the water was poured off. A little fresh water was added, and then we steamed the rice for a few minutes. Well that works pretty good. Seems like we didn't know about frying rice in those days—as that would have been a water saver. One day I used a little fresh water to make some curlew [white ibis] gravy. Well, too little water was used, and the gravy was too thick—commonly called "walking gravy." So Wesley had some unkind words to say about it. When it piles up like horse manure, it's too thick.

Wes did tell me of camping on the Joe River, where we were, in the early part of the twentieth century with his brother-in-law Bill Ashley.[10] Seems at the time they got a fair price for otters and coons during the winter months. Wes said that when he and Bill Ashley were back in that country hunting and trapping, they only had gannets or flintheads to eat. They ate those birds almost everyday. Then one day Bill came back with a deer, and they just threw the old pot of birds overboard.

Maybe they were staying out of town, trying to enjoy the backwoods, since they probably were being harassed by the police because their family was being sought by the law in South Florida.[11] Most of the Ashley-Mobley men were wiped out in 1924 at the Sebastian Bridge. A couple more disappeared while smuggling illegal spirits from Bimini in 1921.

For whatever reason Wes was good to me, for which I was grateful. Wes never spoke of the Ashley gang, except once, when he asked me how far I had ever poled a boat at one time. Whatever I answered, he remarked that he knew of a fellow that had poled a boat for sixty miles in a short time. This was the same distance John Ashley had poled a dugout canoe, loaded with enough otter hides to bring a reported twelve hundred dollars down the New River canal. He sold the pelts at Girtman's store in Miami. This incident occurred after John Ashley's hunting partner, an Indian by the name of Desoto Tiger, had been shot and dropped overboard.[12] Nothing further was said on the subject.

I wish now that I had asked more about his life and happenings. Somehow it didn't seem the thing to do at the time. But he knew plenty, no doubt. Wes would look in the fire for long periods of time as if he was skull-mulling things that had happened over the years, long after I'd gone to bed. Many things have been mulled over by men gazing into the fire, but those days are gone in South Florida—or nearly so.

Man should never write about another's ignorance without doing the same for himself. And I really showed mine one time and was too cowardly to tell about it. I must have been four-fifths grown when camping on the Joe River with Wesley Mobley. To me this was the greatest thing in the world—an ignorant kid to be camping with this old woodsman. Everyday we'd walk the marsh—going our separate ways, splitting up the marsh. Sometimes when coming to the camp, I'd get over on his trail—the last half mile or so. He didn't like that but hadn't said much about it. Everyone that ever knocked around in the lower swamps has heard of large snakes hereabouts.[13] Probably someone started these rumors to have some fun or discourage competition. Coming to camp one evening, I got over on Wes's trail. There was a sign in the trail that at first appeared to be where a seven- or eight-foot gator had crawled. They, like anything or anybody, take the beaten trail. I was looking for his footprints to make sure how big he was. And well, now! I couldn't find any. Now what? Had to be a snake. But he must have been a sambo. I knew if I told Wes about it he would know that I'd been on his trail. The snake's trail went into a pond. That night I asked Wes if he knew of any big snakes. "Why," he asked, "have you seen any sign of one?" "Ooh, no," I lied—but I was sure that he knew by the way he asked me. Anyway, I stayed off his trail.

Much later somebody told me that Wes had drug a tree trunk down his trail and made the snake sign—just to make a fool of me, and that wasn't hard to do.

Years later I used to hunt the Joe River marsh with Buck Rohrer. No one ever had a more capable partner in the swamps than Buck. He was a small, wiry man of 135 pounds and was equal at least as anyone in the swamps of South Florida. He didn't talk a lot but done a lot. Before and after the 1935 storm we pushed glade boats over most of South Florida—wherever there was water deep enough to push pole or wade and drag a glade skiff. We tried to cover it all. Just living and trying to find something to sell, and that was mostly gators and otters.

Before the 1935 storm, we poled two glade skiffs to Camp Nasty close to Oyster Bay about ten miles up Joe River. We had never seen a map, and we called it the South River—a name we got from the natives at Flamingo. There were lots of camps in the Everglades called Camp Nasty. The one on the Joe River was probably named by the Roberts boys. It was called that because the ground was always wet. We usually didn't camp there because it was too open, and everyone knew what you were doing—they could see your boat and camp. The Bill Ashley Camp was close—the same campground that was used with Wes Mobley earlier—so we stayed there two weeks. It had overhanging mangroves where we could hide our boats. We made cabbage frond beds under the cabbage trees. This river was lined with cabbage trees on the western swamp side, beautiful. Now the palms are all gone. The sea has rose enough to kill the palms and put the end on camping.[14] The campground's now a few inches under water, so the sea must be rising. We carried a three-eighths-inch copper coil, a five-gallon galvanized can, and a lard-can suitcase. The lard-can suitcase was used as the condenser, and the steam off the salty water in the five-gallon can went through the copper coil and was turned into fresh water. We only used this method of getting water when the water we carried was running low. The water in the marsh seemed to always have a taint of salt; we tried every pond but drank little of it.

We split up the Joe River Marsh and hunted separately from sun up to nigh sundown. We each took part of the Joe's River Marsh and would fan out in about three-mile stretches. We knew it was about three miles 'cause that was about as far as you could get before giving out and still be able to get back by dark—this being a spongy marsh. Buck always came in after I did and generally had a bigger load. This was the richest marsh I ever seen, everything in South Florida was living there and fat and healthy; we would see deer everyday. Birds were thick, all kinds. We ate well.

We made lots of burns, which made walking easier. After burning, the long, white hearts of the big sawgrass were easy to pull and made good eating. No lunch was carried, as we was hard after something to sell. We'd eat at night. Like I said, Buck Rohrer was hard to beat at swamping but maybe a little unpredictable. After about nine days, when he came in and started his chores of taking care of the skins, he blurted, "Well, I'm ready to go home, gun snapped." I asked, "Where is it? Maybe we can fix it." "Sticking in the mud! Barrel first," he said. And he had no desire to walk that way on the morrow and go to it. After he lost his gun, we hunted together. One of us would kill a gator, then set a fire to signal the other. We'd take turns skinning the gator, then the nonskinning man would walk on.

Even after Buck lost his gun, we stayed in the woods as we had arranged a ride from the Coot Bay Landing at a certain time. So we hunted together for the rest of the trip, never going back to pick up the .22 rifle. When putting together a trip after that I would ask him if he was going back for his .22 that was "sticking in the mud." There was a woman in Buck's life—might of had something to do with him wanting to go home early. Everybody is different.

In Little Madeira at the Time of Pearl Harbor

Buck Rohrer and I had come in to Flamingo and was told about Pearl Harbor. We didn't know about Pearl Harbor for about eight or nine days after the bombing, as we were on a two-week trip from Manatee Creek to Flamingo. Buck's brother, Harvey, drove us on the railroad bed to Manatee Creek. The railroad bed had been cleaned of rails and ties, and it was a rough ride. We launched our glade skiff, which had a one-and-one-half Briggs motor (called a hothead), at Manatee Creek and from there we hunted every creek we came across. We followed the inland waterways and small creeks through Long Sound, Bay Sunday, Snag Bay, Joe Bay, and then Mud Bay until we came into Little Madeira Bay by East Creek ["Eastern Creek Route" on the map included in this volume]. Some of these creeks were tunnels of mangroves, but people kept them cut through. In other places, this route was five feet wide. People used this route, along the inside, if it was bad weather—or if they were looking for something. Sometimes fishermen would come into Joe's Bay looking for silver mullet. We'd usually take several days to make this trip—hunting and camping along the way.

We had a little camp on the west end of Little Madeira Bay that I called the Cabbage Trees Camp. There were lots of cabbage trees then at this spot, and there was a sand beach. In the mangroves, there were a few gators and crocs and deer. From there we walk-hunted the many little ponds and gator holes around the marsh along Little Madeira Bay.[15] It was skeeter ridden, but a good gator marsh, although overhunted. The marsh was kind of north westerly of Little Madeira Bay; it was sawgrass-rugged and with some buttonwood and mangroves. Sometimes we would take a boat into Taylor Creek about a half mile or three-fourths mile and fall back into a strand of the creek that ran westerly. (Both Taylor Creek and East Creek run into Little Madeira Bay.) Taylor Creek was full of mangroves—hard to navigate. From this creek we could get into the first of these ponds or continue on going north and northwesterly. There was probably a resident gator in each of these ponds. You don't see many gators in these small ponds 'cause the big male gators are too territorial. And a sow gator only wants to be with her young until mating season. From the first pond we'd walk-hunt the rest of the ponds in the marsh. I never saw anyone up in that marsh when I was camping there.

When I first hunted this area in about 1931 or 1932, I saw the remnants of a house along the East Creek into Little Madeira Bay. The cement foundations of the house were on the east side of the creek and its mouth. There are big date palms around where the house had been and some old wagon rims. I never did go back to look for that house site, but you probably could still find some of the foundation.

Years later, when I was camping in there with Buck Rohrer, in early December of 1941, we saw a houseboat anchored in the middle of Little Madeira Bay as we came out of Taylor Creek. It was dark, and we were fire-hunting the creek and the bay. As we came out someone from the houseboat put a big spotlight on us. We were lit up like day-light, and it seemed like the light was not going to let up. They kept the light on us, and Buck motioned for me to head toward the houseboat. When we got into talking distance, Buck hollered that if they didn't put out the light that he would. The light went out. It turned out that the houseboat was full of government cotton hunters. The houseboat had little boats tied to it so the cotton hunters could go ashore and look for the wild cotton. Had we known that it was a government houseboat, we would have left without saying anything—since they could have made trouble for us since we was hunting gators. However, we were in our rights as Monroe County was still open to hunting reptiles. Maybe they thought we was Japanese. We seemed to have trouble wherever we went.

A few days later we stopped at Flamingo and were told about Pearl Harbor. I had been examined in 1940 and put in 4-F. The doctor said I could never be put in service because of my health. But after Pearl Harbor, I was put in 1-A and was in the army at twenty-six years old, making twenty-one dollars a month. A year of misery and butchery, and I was turned out with more troubles than when I went in, but God what a pleasure to be free again.

Hurricanes

The hurricane that hit the Keys on Labor Day in 1935 changed the way the Cape and Flamingo looked for years.[16] Before this hurricane, west of Flamingo way down in there before you get to the East Cape Canal, there was a huge group of black mangrove trees that the locals called the "Black Woods."[17] Before the storm, I never found much dead wood in there. Afterward, you could get all the wood you needed

Debris hanging off a dead black mangrove a few years after the Labor Day Hurricane of 1935. Courtesy Alexander Sprunt IV.

for building smokes—the large black mangroves were all dead. When this hurricane hit, all the houses on Flamingo were wiped out.

Other storms had hit Flamingo before. Living there, out in the open, it was just a way of life. The land was no more than six or eight inches above high tide, trouble was expected. Before the hurricane in 1910, they grew sugarcane on the prairie, a little further west just on the edge of Flamingo—'cause there was more shell on the ground.[18] At Flamingo it was all mud. Syrup making was profitable around the Flamingo area when the railroad was being built. The old-timers said that the sugarcane there turned out a lot of syrup. After the syrup was made, it was hauled on a sailboat to Key West and sold. My mother

Mangroves along the East Cape Canal destroyed in the 1935 Labor Day storm, 1938. Courtesy Alexander Sprunt IV.

told me that you could get a real good price for syrup and vegetables in Key West before they put the railroad through.

The 1910 hurricane knocked out all of the sugarcane on and around Flamingo. The land was all salted up from the storm surge. Ain't no doubt this was a treacherous place to live and make a living. After the storm, Louis Loudon and Loren Roberts went along the west coast looking for cane sprouts to replant. They went around looking for new cane, probably around the Watsons' place. He got killed in 1910, you know, just after the storm.[19] How much they planted, I don't know. After the railroad got put in to Key West, the trade slowed because most everything was shipped by rail.

I was living on the Long Glade, near Homestead, when the Labor Day storm hit in 1935. It wasn't a large storm, but it was powerful. Except for some wind and rain, we didn't know much about the disaster that happened on the Keys until afterward. A few days after the sure enough bad hurricane, I was approached by the Homestead fire chief to guard a fire engine that was housed under the Matecumbe Hotel. Seems like Homestead had some kind of hold on that fire engine, and they needed someone to watch it. They asked me to watch the fire engine because they knew I did a lot of camping, and they thought I might like to work for two weeks. The pay was two dollars a day.

At the time, the fire station and the police station were in the same building in Homestead. I told the fire chief that I would take the job but that I had to be back in two weeks. A partner and I had a young tomato seedbed in the pinelands that we had to plant in two weeks. Everything was agreed to by all parties.

The fire chief and two or three others took me down in David Barnes' Chevrolet as far as Snake Creek along the highway to the Keys. The road to Homestead from Snake Creek was cleared off, as they were using it to haul the bodies from the Keys. This storm killed about four hundred people. For a few days, the WPA and the National Guard were bringing the dead people into Homestead until they got so rotten that they were running out of the boxes and things. Then they started burning them there at Islamorada and other sites. That country was in a terrible mess.

The damage started getting a little bit worse as you went down after Tavernier Creek, but it was nothing like it was on Islamorada. At Snake Creek the bridge, including the railroad bridge, was completely washed out. All the boats that the National Guard and the WPA were using to haul things and people to and from the Keys were stationed at Snake Creek. There must have been about twenty-five people there. Lots of people donated their cabin boats to the cleanup effort, and we took a boat from Snake Creek to Islamorada. It's been so long, but I think it couldn't have been over ten miles.

After we got to Islamorada, I stowed my stuff, and we made our way on foot to the Matecumbe Hotel. There were no houses left there, and all the mangroves were torn up and beat down. Everything was covered with seaweed and old lumber. The railroad was all torn up, and the rails had washed into the water. The fire engine I was to guard was under the fallen-in hotel. We got it out and pushed it maybe a mile to Islamorada. After uncovering the fire engine, we noticed that the brass bell was missing. It was found among some men, and they said that the National Guard were using it for tolling the dead. The ones in charge of the fire engine took it into town.

The WPA workers would come everyday by boat and look for bodies. I remember that if the wind was blowing and I was down wind from the burning bodies, the smell would wake you up. At night, I would walk the road sometimes to get away from the smell. It was said that the workers would cook crayfish in garbage cans; rumor was that bodies found floating would have many crayfish eating them. This was not seen by me.

In those days we never heard the word "lobster," as the crackers called them crawfish; and the Conchs used the "y" in speaking of crayfish. But with the overflow of Yankees, the word "lobster" took over. I had hopes years ago (and they didn't last long) that the skeeters and hurricanes would run the Yankees out of here, but it just about happened the other way around.

Where the veteran's camp had been—not far from where I was camped on Matecumbe—there was hundreds of canned goods piled along the railway bed. These cans had no labels after the beating they took in the storm. They were much better groceries than what I had brought with me from town. I soon learned that by shaking them that I could pretty much tell what they was. I even found some army shoes and clothes that were better than mine. I was just a kid then, nineteen years old, and the whole trip seemed like some kind of nightmare.

The men from Homestead assured me before they left that they would come back for me in two weeks. They did not pick me up when they promised. Low-down people. That made me a liar to my partner. However, I caught a boat out one day after the agreed time. I met only one man that had weathered the storm and stayed on there afterward. I believe his name was Leo Johnson. Before I got on the crowded boat at Snake Creek, I stored my gear under Johnson's wrecked house (we called gear "suggens," a word I learned from my grandma). It was several months before I got back there, and everything was ruined as another light storm had got everything wet.

*   *   *

About ten years later, Flamingo was hit by another storm. My wife and I had made our way into Little Cattail Lake, during the mid–1940s in October. We hunted the Cattail Lakes several times a year and usually expected to stay four or five days. I had built a little flat-bottomed boat, which we attached a one-cylinder motor to. We towed our glade skiff behind the motorboat through Lake Ingraham to Little Sable Creek. We usually hid the motorboat at the creek and continued into Little Cattail Lake on the skiff.

The first night we were there, the wind blew, and the lake water was shaking so hard that the gators wouldn't hold fire. The combination of the choppy water and the bouncing motion of the boat will usually scare a gator. The wind blew continually for the next few days and nights, while a light rain fell. We were not doing well so we stayed out of the Big Cattail Lake. Finally, one late evening, we headed back to Flamingo. Before we got into the bay, the dark came upon us; it was still raining and blowing. The night was tar black. Since we couldn't see the shore, we tried to guide ourselves from the East Cape Canal along the Gulf to Flamingo using the wind. As it had blown from the same direction for days, we figured it wouldn't change now. The Gulf was very rough, and the wind was gusty. We ran the boat for about an hour and a half and then headed a little north—hoping to see a light at Flamingo. I stopped once to roll a cigarette. My wife never forgave me for that.

We finally saw a light and headed for it. Some people in a boat heard the motor popping and waved a lantern. It was my old friend Kay Irwin. He told us to get what we wanted from our house and head up the canal to the Coot Bay Hammock since a hurricane was almost upon us.[20] The people at Flamingo always went to the Coot Bay Hammock to ride out a storm, Kay said. It was two miles from Flamingo, and there was a dirt road then along the canal that led to the hammock.

Everyone else had gone ahead with their boats. In another hour, we would have been in the storm as the wind was beginning to strengthen. We grabbed a few clothes and headed up the canal. My wife drove our Model A Ford to the hammock while I took our boats there in the canal. The old-timers knew the storm was coming, and the weather report said the wind would probably be only seventy-five miles per hour, I was told. At Flamingo, a few people listened to the news on battery-operated radios.

Anyway, wouldn't you know it? Before we could get settled to put up with what the night would bring, two women with a baby begged us to take them into town. They were crying, and as I had the only vehicle that might make it to town, I had to take them. I couldn't say no. After Kay Irwin said he would take care of our boats and things, my wife and I headed toward Homestead with the women. Instead of taking the Ingraham Highway, we took the Rowdy Bend Road. This road was built by cotton hunters and intersected with the Ingraham Highway at the Snake Bight Canal; because the cotton pickers maintained the road, it was usually in better shape than the Ingraham Highway. The Model A felt its way through the muddy road by staying in

Glen's house at Flamingo, made from a converted houseboat, 1947.

the deep ruts. I thought the best way to get into town was by following the Rowdy Bend Road. Well it didn't turn out to be that good of a choice. The only time I make a mistake is when I go to do something.

After about a mile or so on Rowdy Bend, we ended up nose down in the ditch. The storm was showing off pretty good by now, and we started to walk back. We couldn't see anything, so we had to feel our way along that muddy road. The wind and the rain felt like needles hitting you. My wife toted the woman's baby, and I carried our cat inside my shirt. Now as my friend Oman Barber would say, the cat was "being excused" inside my shirt. Well, we threw away the shirt and kept the cat. About two miles and two hours later, we arrived at the Coot Bay Hammock. The heavy hammock foiled most of the wind. The men had cut and were cooking swamp cabbage and canned corn beef and cornbread for the fifteen to twenty people who were there. One of my greatest pleasures was knowing these men, especially the Irwins. What other men could or would cook a meal like that on a buttonwood fire in the middle of a storm?

The next day we went back to Flamingo and found quite a mess. Our house had moved north about a quarter mile and became lodged in the buttonwoods. At the time, we lived in an old houseboat that we put up on the ground. This house was about the size of the Ochopee Post Office—about 7' x 10'. I was liberal in them days as the man only asked ten dollars for the house, and I gave him twenty. Nowadays, with all my flea market dickering experience, I would try to buy the houseboat for seven.

During the storm, the water must have rose four or five feet as the house was full of fish and mud. Seaweed had lodged into our mattress springs and inside of our stove. Sometime later we put poles under the house, like a sled, and pulled it out with a big fish truck. In August of 1947, when the word got out that the park was coming we gave the house to Kay Irwin and left.

Instructions for Building
a Glade Skiff

In the sixty years that Glen Simmons has been building glade skiffs, he has never relied upon any formal boat plans. The following instructions represent an attempt to translate his intuitive process into standardized building guidelines. Glen advises the future builder to modify the following plans as needed.

Materials:

Two pieces of 8-foot, 1/4" marine plywood (or one 16-foot marine plywood board, which is preferable)
Two 5/8" x 10" x 14' cypress boards (for sides)
One 1–1/4" x 6" x 22" cypress board (for stern)
If cypress is unavailable, use white cedar, redwood, or red cedar
#12 solid copper wire (can be stripped from electrical house wire)
Copper carpet tacks
Five-penny copper nails

Fiberglass (light-weight matting)
Epoxy resin
Tools:
Two 1/2" x 13" angle irons
18" threaded rod, 1/4" in diameter
Two wing nuts to fit over threaded rod
Fine wood rasp
10 gauge electrical cord
Wide hook (a wooden hook is best)
Heavy flat pliers
Wood plane
Hammer

Preparing Plywood for Skiff's Bow and Bottom

1. Examine the plywood pieces, determine for each board: (a) the best 34" in width, and (b) which side should face inside (has the most patched places etc.).

2. Cut each plywood piece to 34" in width.

3. Work off the centerline of this 34" width to cut out the rest of the boat. Glen snaps a chalk line down the center of each piece of plywood (measuring 17" in from edges). Later, the chalk line will help align the two pieces of plywood when they are spliced.

Cut Out Skiff Bottom

1. Cut out aft section of skiff bottom (Board 1 in diagram), according to the measurements in diagram. Set aside.

2. Use the chalk line to measure out 26" for the splice-end of Board 2 (Line A in diagram). The bow-end of Board 2 is also 26" wide; again use center chalk line to measure this out. From each side of the bow, measure back 30" at an angle until these lines intersect the sides (Lines C and D in diagram). Lines C and D should be symmetrical about the center line. Cut out Board 2 according to these measurements.

3. From center of bow-end, make a 24" cut along chalk line of Board 2 (Line B). From bow-end of Line B, mark off 4" along center cut (to Point E in diagram).

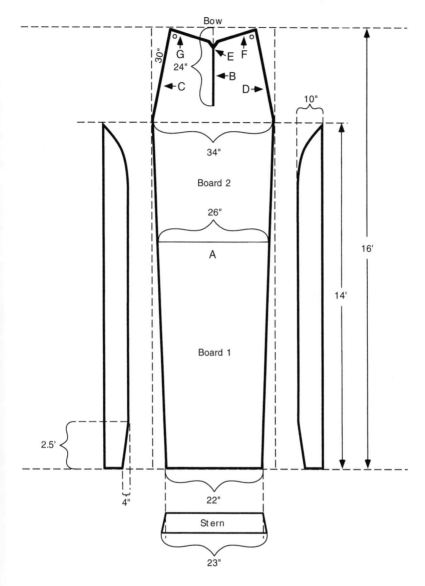

Plans for building a glade skiff.

4. To form bow (Lines F and G in diagram), draw a line from Point E to each corner of bow. As shown in the diagram, these lines are slightly curved at Point E, then become straight after a few inches. The lines need to be straight as the angle clamp, used for pulling the bow together, must fit tightly against them. Glen suggests cutting one side and then using it as a pattern to cut the other—as they must be completely symmetrical or the bow will not be straight.

5. After bow lines have been cut, the insides are slightly beveled with a fine wood rasp. Prior to planing bow lines, decide which side of the board will be used as the inside of the boat. The lines are beveled on the inside of Board 2 and are relative to the 90-degree angle defined by both edges of the bow, when seen in cross section. This planing is gradual and is minimal at Point E (the bottom of the bow) and becomes more pronounced toward bow-end. Glen suggests beginning at Point E, taking off only the first layer of plywood, then graduate this planing until reaching the end of Lines F and G where the planed angle should be sharper.

6. Bore holes (to fit the threaded rod) at 1 1/2" in and back from the top of the bow of Board 2 (at the end of F and G). When the bow is finally constructed, this hole is used for the bow line.

Building the Bow

Glen uses a homemade clamp, made of two angle irons, to pull the bow together. The angle irons are fastened together at the bottom with a small bolt and face outward so that the flat edges fit against the split bow. A 1/4" threaded rod, held in place with wing nuts, is used to tighten the angle clamp.

1. Soak the bow-end of Board 2, about the first three feet of it, in water for two or three days until bow can be pulled together without breaking or cracking (longer if weather is cold).

2. While soaking, assemble homemade angle clamp. Bore holes at the top of each angle iron to fit threaded rod. Hold the angle irons together at the opposite end with a small bolt. Angle clamp will be fit against the bow (Lines F and G) so flat sides should be facing in. Glen holds the angle clamp in place with 10 gauge electrical wire tied to the

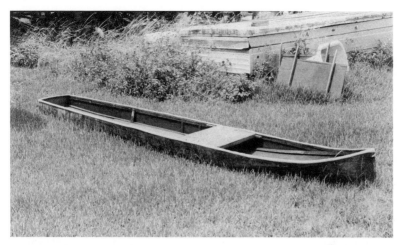

A thirty-five-year-old glade skiff built by Glen.

bottom (bolted end) of the angle clamp, which is then hooked at the center of the splice-end of Board 2. Use a wide hook to attach angle-clamp cord to the splice-end of Board 2 so it will not scar the wood. The wire/line that holds the angle clamp in place runs from the bow of the boat, under the plywood, to the splice-end of Board 2.

3. After Board 2 is ready to be bent, put angle clamp in place. Put 1/4" threaded rod through holes at bow and angle clamp, with wing nuts. The electrical wire holding the clamp in place must be taut so the angle clamp doesn't fall off. Tighten the angle clamp with the wing nuts along the threaded rod until Lines F and G come together. If you have difficulty pulling the bow together, Glen suggests soaking the wood longer. An assistant may be helpful during this stage. One person can hold bow together, while the other tightens the angle clamp along the threaded rod.

4. When bow has been pulled together, bore holes about 1/2" apart along the outside of the angle clamp. The holes need to fit the #12 copper wire, which is used to suture the bow together. Start boring these holes at the top of bow, and putting copper wire in each hole. Cut the wire so that about 1/4" hangs over on each side after threaded through holes. Pull the wire pieces together with pliers and bury the wire into the wood. When finished, there will be about fifteen of these

Doug and Don Edwards splicing a skiff bottom in Glen's barn.

sutured places. Glen says that the more the wire is buried the better the boat will look later.

5. After the bow is held together with the copper wire, take off the angle clamp. The bow may need to be planed a little—be careful not to cut the copper wire. When the bow is perfect, fiberglass the bow, inside and outside. A strip of fiberglass on the inside and outside will hold it, and it will never leak (lightweight matting will do).

Splicing the Bottom of the Boat

Scarf Boards 1 and 2 together. Glen suggests planing the splice-ends of each board back an inch, at angles, so they can be overlapped on top of each other. Although it doesn't look as smooth, Glen has, on occasion, simply butted the two boards together and then put a scab over the inside seam. Glen glues the joint with epoxy. When dry, tack and brad scarf together with copper carpet tacks. When the boat is completed, fiberglass this joint. Splicing the bottom together can be avoided by using a 16-foot piece of plywood (this is advisable).

Attaching the Transom and Sides

Attaching the sides of the boat to the bow and bottom is the most difficult part of building the skiff. You will find that when you try to attach the sideboards to the bow that it will take a lot of planing to get them to fit. Because each boat is different, Glen's only advice is to keep working at it until one side is right. Then use that board as a pattern for the other.

1. The cypress boards used for the boat's sides need to be cut and planed so they are exactly alike. The best way to ensure that the sides are the same is to cut one board to fit the boat, clamp it to the other board, and use it for a model. Also, plane the boards before cutting so that they are both flat.

2. Glen suggests laying one board against the side of the boat, leaving an extra inch toward the bow. The sides fit into the boat beginning about 30" back from the bow.

3. Measure and cut the first board to fit the bow end of the skiff and to produce a 4" lift at the stern (angle to produce this lift begins about 2.5' forward from the stern—as in diagram).

4. Clamp boards together and use the already cut board as a model for cutting the second. Plane the outside edges of the cypress boards to fit skiff bottom and bow. The planed angle should be most pronounced at the point where the sides meet the bow.

5. Bore holes in the cypress boards before nailing sides in place. Copper nails should be placed about an inch apart.

6. The transom goes in last. Use copper nails for this also. Glen also puts small wooden braces on the inside of the transom to keep it secure. The stern board should be tilted out at a slight angle.

Finishing the Boat

1. The boat's gunwale should be 4" or 5" wide at the bow of the boat and continue at this width past where the sides intersect the bow. The gunwale continues as a narrower band around both sides of the boat. Glen makes it out of plywood. Use copper nails to secure it.

2. The seat of the boat should be placed about a third of the way back from the bow.

3. Glen sometimes constructs an optional poling platform at the aft-end of the skiff.

N O T E S

Preface

1. Of course, Glen's experiences offer an Anglo-European interpretation of Everglades life, rather than that of the Seminole people who hunted and camped the Everglades during the same period. Kersey's *Pelts, Plumes, Hides* (1975) offers a comprehensive analysis of the Seminole hide trade in the Everglades for the same period.

2. Although the United States Geographical Board decreed that the spelling of this swamp would be "Okefenokee," Francis Harper preferred "Oke-finokee" —as the name was derived from the Creek word *O-ke-fin-o-cau* (Harper and Presley 1981, xv).

Chapter 1: The Long Glade

1. Frank C. Craighead Sr. refers to the interrelationship between animals and plants around an alligator pond as a "gator hole ecosystem" (1971, xi). Small ponds are maintained by alligators; they literally keep the ponds wallowed-out throughout the year. During the dry season, the aquatic life

in these ponds provides a feeding ground for birds, turtles, rabbits, panthers, and other species (Robertson 1988, 9).

2. In many instances, Glen uses the terms "river" and "slough" interchangeably, as sloughs provide the main drainage channels for much of the Everglades complex.

3. In South Florida, the term "hammock" refers to a tree island, found in the open pinewoods, in the Everglades or along parts of the coast. Usually occupying an area of higher elevation, hammocks are seldom flooded and enjoy some natural protection from fire (Robertson 1988, 12).

4. Craighead notes that prior to drainage efforts in the 1920s, these small creeks, such as the Wink Eye, provided a necessary source of freshwater to the almost "landlocked" mangrove area east of the Shark River (1964, 40). A map included in the article cited above shows the location of the Wink Eye Creek.

5. The Last Chance Saloon is located on the west side of US 1 where the highway leaves Florida City and heads south to the Florida Keys.

6. Where Glen had to pole through only a hundred yards of mangroves, there are now one to two miles of mangroves—which have moved inland, primarily since the 1940s because of reduced freshwater flow (perhaps stemming from the building of the Florida East Coast Railway and later the highway to the Florida Keys) and the documented rise in sea levels along Florida shorelines.

7. The Camp Jackson Trail led from Goulds through the glade, passing what was later Homestead at the end of Mowry Street, and down to Camp Jackson near Royal Palm Hammock, later called Paradise Key. Camp Jackson was named by William Krome for the U.S. surveyor who charted South Florida in 1848. Camp Jackson became Krome's permanent camp while he was surveying for the Florida East Coast Railway Company in 1902. Krome was exploring an alternate route for the Key West Extension of the Florida East Coast Railway through the Everglades to Cape Sable and then across Florida Bay (Taylor, 143).

8. If the dead alligator remained under the cold water, the hide would stay preserved for a day or two. Although the carcass would obviously smell, the hide could still be salvaged. But if the alligator floated to the surface and stayed in the sun for as much as fifteen minutes, its scales would begin to come off. Gator hunters called this "slipping."

9. The prehistoric Calusa, who lived on Florida's southwest coast between the Caloosahatchee River and the Cape Sable region, built high mounds that served as elevations for monuments and villages as well as for burial purposes and kitchen middens. These kitchen middens, also called shell

mounds, served as repositories for the community's rufuse. Shells, pottery, and tools are often found in these mounds, which reached astonishing heights after many years of use.

10. Glen's father was undoubtedly "uneasy" living in the Ten Thousand Islands because of its reputation as a refuge for outlaws and fugitives. The 1939 WPA publication *Florida: A Guide to the Southernmost State* offers this description of life in the region: "Feuds between groups are not uncommon; nets are destroyed, houses and boats burned, and many killings occur in disputes over claims to fishing grounds. Channel markers placed by the Government have been repeatedly destroyed by natives who fear poachers" (1939, 411).

11. The folk expression "knew his onions" was popular in the 1920s and suggested capability. The slang phrase was used in one of the Burma-Shave roadside advertisements of the era and went, "You Know Your Onions, Lettuce Suppose, This Beets 'Em All, Don't Turnip Your Nose, Burma-Shave" (Rowsome 1965, 81).

12. These "rice birds" were bobolinks, a migratory bird that are in South Florida from August through September and again from late April through early May.

13. Purslane is a common garden weed that has been domesticated and is prepared like other greens.

14. This dairy was located beyond what was then called the Horse Head Corner, which is where the road which leads to the main entrance of the park (SR 9336) abruptly curves west after heading south from Palm Drive. About a hundred yards from this curve, a rock finger (or rocky pineland) intersected the glade. A road ran down this rock finger, and the dairy was located at the end. Glen believes the dairy closed in 1929.

15. Land sales were so rapid during the boom years that small deposits (usually 10 percent of the property's value) were placed as binders, or options, for land in exchange for the ownership papers. A substantially higher payment was then due in thirty days or less. These land speculators, or so-called "binder boys," would then resell the bound property at a much greater profit to someone else, with only ever-increasing binders exchanging hands. The frenzied accumulation of binders and their brisk turnover partially account for the period's great inflation (George 1986, 35). When land values dramatically dropped in 1926, speculators left with multiple binders, in most cases, faced immediate financial ruin.

16. Gladesmen referred to prohibition officers as "prohis." During the '20s, '30s, and '40s, hunters used fifty-pound or one hundred–pound metal lard cans, which cost about ten cents at local grocery stores, as suitcases. They

usually took two of these cans with them on glades trips. One held clothes and bedding; food and some dry grass used for starting fires were carried in the other.

Chapter 2: Everglades Backcountry Camps

1. Hikers and bicyclists can still travel along what remains of the old Ingraham Highway for about eleven miles (it is clearly marked on maps that are available at the Everglades National Park's Main Visitor Center). The current Main Park Road follows the route of the Ingraham Highway from Sweet Bay Pond to Flamingo.

2. As Glen describes later in this section, gladesmen, particularly deer hunters, used controlled burning as a hunting technique. After the glades or mangroves were burned, deer and other wildlife became attracted to the burned area's new growth. A. W. Dimock describes hunters using burning as a technique in the late 1800s: "Sometimes a hunter drags a torch of palmetto fans across the wind, through the grass of prairie until it is swept by a wall of roaring flame, half a mile in width. Turkeys are unharmed; deer are even attracted by the ashes; but snakes perish by the thousand in the flames" (1926, 257). Anglo hunters may have adopted this controlled burning technique from the Seminoles. Kersey quotes Charles Cory's *Hunting and Fishing* (1896), which describes Seminoles using burning when hunting: "The Indians burn the country every spring in a most reckless manner, destroying great quantities of timber. They set the dry grass on fire, so that, by destroying the old grass, the new, fresh shoots coming up attract the deer and turkeys, which are generally found on such places. Besides this, the ground being burned off renders still-hunting much more easy, for the game can be so much more readily seen" (1971, 47).

3. Later, in the 1960s, the Reef was renamed the "Buttonwood Embankment" by Dr. Frank C. Craighead Sr. Glen Simmons served as Dr. Craighead's guide while he explored this region. Called the Reef by locals, the Buttonwood Embankment is a higher ridge of land lying to the north of West, Cuthbert, and Seven Palm Lakes and running along the edge of the Saline Mangrove Zone. As Craighead notes, the Buttonwood Embankment "serves as a levee impounding the freshwater glades to the north. It continues across the Park, broken in places, on the inner bank of the string of lakes and bays, and along the small tributaries pushing into the saw grass of the Freshwater Swamps" (Craighead 1971, 120).

4. Ed Brooker's camp is in what is now called the Whiskey Creek area of Everglades National Park.

5. The term "fire-hunt" refers to hunting at night while using a carbide lantern; see chapter 3.

6. Within the local community, moonshiners had a particularly bad reputation. Glen's reticence is mirrored in A. W. Dimock's description of an encounter with moonshiners in the Everglades backcountry in the late 1800s. In his rather humorous account, Dimock (an environmental advocate and writer) describes coming upon the moonshiners, saying, "Some of the whispered colloquy which we overheard was unprintable and the tension was only relieved when it was understood that the boxes we carried contained camera and sensitive plates" (1926, 77). Apparently Dimock's audacity appealed to the moonshiners, whose confidence was gained after his party sampled the "fiery potation, straight from the still" (1926, 78).

7. Nobles Still was a popular camp and landing site located just northeast of and on the opposite side of the Ingraham Highway from the Hell's Bay Trail. According to Glen, the landing was named after Bill Nobles, who ran a whiskey still in the hammock during Prohibition and owned a grocery store in the southwest section of Homestead. Currently the Noble Hammock Canoe Trail (note spelling difference) is a three-mile loop that is maintained by the National Park Service.

8. Argyle Hendry was a well-known Everglades character, renowned equally for his crocodile-hunting skills and his curmudgeonly demeanor. Hendry was hired in 1942 by W. E. Dickinson of the Milwaukee Public Museum to get a crocodile specimen for the museum's display. With great restraint, Dickinson discusses this expedition, saying only, "It was evident that he [Hendry] had done little in anticipation of our arrival, although he did have a 5 1/2- or 6-foot crocodile under his pier. It was tethered by a rope around its snout" (1953, 153). Dickinson describes Hendry's technique for catching a live crocodile, including the unusual step of dismantling the boat so the floorboards could be used to blockade the crocodile in its cave (1953, 153).

9. Palm Hammock, now the site of the Royal Palm visitor center within the national park, was a well-known reference point for local hunters, naturalists, and explorers. The area to the west of the hammock, which was farmed along the Big Bend Road, was simply referred to as "Below the Hammock."

10. According to Glen, other local names for great blue herons include scoggins, blue johns, wauk-a-chobee, Johnny-one-guts, and go-slows.

11. That hide buyer was Henry Coppinger. In the early 1900s, a number of Seminole Indians lived at Coppinger's Tropical Gardens on NW Seventh

Street in Miami. Covington notes that by 1918, Seminoles were selling live baby gators and stuffed small alligators to tourists, shipping hides to northern factories, and presenting alligator wrestling and Seminole-style weddings to visitors at Coppinger's gardens (Covington 1993, 190–91).

12. Kersey mentions Charlie Billie in his overview of the 1934 *Miami Daily News*'s investigation by Cecil R. Warren that focused on the living conditions of Seminole Indians. Warren interviewed Charlie Billie's son, Chestnut Billie, who said that his father had "not had the care that he gives his camp. His right arm hangs useless. The forearm is broken and has remained unset for 10 years. Whether the old fracture will heal or not is now doubtful. No white man has offered to aid him. He is willing to have a white doctor fix it, if he can. . . ."(Kersey 1989, 62).

13. Five-year-old James "Skeegie" Bailey Cash Jr. was kidnapped on the evening of May 29, 1938, from his Princeton, Florida, home in the Redland district. His father, James Cash Sr., complied with the ransom note, which requested that he toss ten thousand dollars in small bills from his car window along a "lonely road" at 4 A.M. near his home, according to a *Miami Daily News* article (1938, A1). The Cash kidnapping led to a massive multiforce manhunt, with members of the state WPA, an eight hundred–man local posse, and the FBI joining forces. After days passed without finding the boy, J. Edgar Hoover arrived from Washington, D.C., to take over the search effort. Twenty-one-year-old Franklin Pierce McCall, who had initially "discovered" the ransom note and participated in the search, was eventually arrested for the crime on June 3. McCall then led investigators to the boy's body, which lay unburied within a half mile of the Cash home.

14. While there are numerous descriptions of the famed Cuthbert Lake region, notably Helen Cruickshank's *Flight into Sunshine* (1948), Frank Chapman's turn-of-the-century narrative parallels other explorers' first impressions:

> At intervals, these shaded passages opened into lakes, six in all, varying in size from a quarter of a mile to between two and three miles in length. The larger lakes were set with islands, breaking the distance and forming charming vistas all bordered with mangroves. Here, still lingered hundreds of Coots and Lesser Scaup Ducks with a few Blue-winged Teal. Here, too, were numerous fish; a bass and a small tarpon leaped into one of our boats as voluntary contributions to our larder. (1908, 140)

The Cuthbert Lake area, including neighboring lakes and marshes, was once famed for its remoteness and abundance of bird life, but the area appears dramatically different today. A channel was cut between West Lake, Long Lake (called East Lake by Glen), and Cuthbert Lake in the mid–1950s. Craighead suggests that this channel allowed salt water to reach the western end of West Lake and therefore endangered a rich winter feeding ground for numerous birds (1971, 6). Glen feels that the introduction of this channel had relatively little impact on the water flow between the lakes, as there were always boat passages between the lakes during his time.

15. When "pole-hunting," a hunter stands above an alligator cave and pushes a long iron pole through the cave's top until he locates the alligator's position. This process is described in detail in chapter 3.

16. East Lake is now called Long Lake.

17. Glen's use of the term "cotton pickers" refers to workers hired by the U.S. Department of Agriculture, Bureau of Entomology and Plant Quarantine, to eradicate wild cotton (*Gossypium hirsutun* L.) in South Florida. Working from a camp at Flamingo, the cotton eradicators built a network of roads to facilitate this process throughout the coastal region of what is now Everglades National Park (as well as beyond the park's current boundaries). The purpose of this project was to prevent the spread of the red cotton borer, which was considered a threat to the commercial cotton crops to the north of Florida (Beard 1938, 60).

18. Glen is referring to people living along the west coast of Florida, particularly around Everglades City.

19. A "skeeter" is a car that has been cut down and made into a truck.

20. What Glen and his contemporaries called the "Yappos" or "Yappo Strand" is a part of the Miami rock ridge where the ridge begins to taper off and break apart. Craighead describes the geology of this region as follows: "Much of this slope is a rough, rocky county of pinnacle rock with islands of pine and hammock growth and numerous ponds and small sloughs intermixed. The rocky area forms the eastern bank of the Shark River Slough, and is crossable by airboat only at a few places and only at maximum water levels" (1971, 50). Important is the fact that Craighead visited this region with Glen after the many large stands of pines, which grew on the Yappo Islands, had burned away.

21. William B. Robertson Jr. in a report to the U.S. Department of the Interior, produced a history of fires in South Florida based upon anecdotal description and newspaper accounts spanning the years 1909 to 1952 (1953, 96). Although Glen is fairly sure the fire that burned the Yappos occurred either in 1934 or 1935, Roberton's report does not include a description of a large fire in the southern Everglades for those years.

22. The Pine Island that Glen refers to should not be confused with Long Pine Key, which is located approximately four miles past the Entrance Station to Everglades National Park.

23. The Pine Island shelf is located approximately four miles past the Everglades National Park gate on the old Context Road (288th Street).

24. Glen walked to the Oak Trees Camp from Lucille Road, then called Frambeau Road by the locals.

Chapter 3: The Hide Trade

1. This quote is found in William Bartram's 1794 *Travels Through North and South Carolina, Georgia, East and West Florida.* Quoted in Vaughn L. Glasgow, *A Social History of the American Alligator* (New York: St. Martin's Press, 1991), 19.

2. Allen and Neill, in the journal *Herpetologica,* report hunters during the 1940s receiving much higher prices for alligator hides. According to their records, for instance, hide hunters averaged more than fifteen dollars for a seven-foot hide in 1942—which was more than double the price Glen received (Allen and Neill 1949, 109).

3. Alligator homes, called "gator holes," are found within any depression in the limestone of the Everglades' shallow marshes where fresh water collects. Alligators maintain these holes by routing out the plants and accumulated thick muck, a mixture of marl and organic matter. During the dry season, water remains within these gator holes that serve as essential reservoirs for the aquatic life of the Everglades (Craighead 1968).

4. The Florida Federation of Women's Clubs led the effort to establish a state park at Palm Hammock (on an inland island called Paradise Key), the current site of the Royal Palm Hammock in Everglades National Park. On November 22, 1916, Royal Palm State Park was dedicated and initially spanned approximately two thousand acres (Jennings 1916, 10). Under the federation's oversight, a lodge was built at the site in 1919, and paths were laid throughout the hammock. The Royal Palm State Park became a federally recognized conservation area in 1934.

5. When Glen is explaining the "run" of the alligator's cave, he means the direction that the cave or den has been dug into the marsh or peat.

6. Chekika, formerly Chekika State Recreational Area, became part of Everglades National Park in 1991. This 640 acres of sawgrass marsh and hardwood tropical hammock was named after Chief Chekika, a famous Seminole leader who was hanged by Col. William Harney in 1840.

7. Big alligators were called "salt-burners" by gladesmen since it took so much salt to cure their hides after they were skinned.

8. The Everglades Station, located thirteen miles south of Florida City, was the last mainland watering stop for the Key West Extension of the Florida East Coast Railway. A freshwater creek crossed the railroad tracks and canal, the fill from which was used for the track's foundations, at the Everglades Station. The creek, which eventually ran into Manatee Bay, was plugged at the Everglades Station to prevent tidal flow from contaminating this freshwater source. The water from the creek was then stored in tanks at the Glades Station and used on the trains (some of which were steam powered).

9. The beam from the carbide lantern would usually confuse the alligator. The term "holding fire" meant that the alligator would remain within the beam's light, instead of sinking to the bottom of the pond.

10. Little West Lake is now named Little Fox Lake.

11. The gator-rod fern was not a specific fern. Any sturdy fern found growing around an alligator's pond would be used in the skinning process.

12. Only the softer underbelly of the alligator was used in a flatskin hide; two longitudinal incisions were made on each side of the belly to remove it. When the entire skin was used, for a hornback hide, one longitudinal incision was made along the mid-ventral line.

13. Reese, quoting a 1902 U.S. Bureau of Fisheries report, notes that these "buttons" on alligator hides were also called "corn marks." According to Reese, these buttons result from "imbedded horn-like tissues" in the center of the alligator's scales. Because these buttons were found more often on alligators in Florida, skins from Florida were, at the time of the report, the "cheapest" on the market (Reese 1915, 29).

14. According to Kersey, the Indian village owned by Egbert L. Lasher was started originally by a Seminole Indian named Willie Willie in 1919. Willie Willie and his father, Charlie Willie, initially owned a successful store near the New River where they charged tourists to view Seminoles living on the grounds. This site was so popular that in 1919 Willie Willie moved his operation to the Miami Musa Isle attraction. Apparently Bert Lasher gained control of the Musa Isle location in 1923 (Kersey 1989, 43). As Kersey notes, Lasher's reputation was tinged by a reported criminal record and later by charges of fraud brought by Willie Willie's widow, Elizabeth, against him. These charges were subsequently investigated by the Department of Justice and Federal Bureau of Investigation (Kersey 1989, 44).

15. Les and Wilfred Piper owned the Everglades Wonder Gardens in Bonita Springs, Florida. In the late 1930s until 1953, they bought live crocodiles that were captured in South Florida, primarily from Key Largo and the Cape Sable region (Behler 1978, 26).
16. The Gum Slough is in the southern part of the Big Cypress National Preserve.
17. The tick eradication program began as a joint federal-state effort to rid the cattle in the southern states of the tropical tick *Boophilus annulatus,* variety *australis* (Kersey, 1989, 124). The state legislature authorized Florida's participation in this program in 1923. These ticks penetrated the cattle's hide, ruining its commercial value, and caused a fever of the spleen (Kersey 1989, 125).
18. The remainder, or nondeveloped portion, of the Allapattah Flats lie in Martin County, east of Lake Okeechobee.

Chapter 4: Flamingo and the Cape

1. Flamingo's most famous resident was Uncle Steve Roberts. Roberts arrived at Flamingo in 1901; he and his descendants were associated closely with the community until 1947, when Flamingo became incorporated into the national park (Tebeau 1963, 109). On a visit to Flamingo in 1919, W. S. Blatchley recalls dining at the Roberts' house with Dr. King of the East Cape Club House saying,

> At Flamingo the principal building is the home of Uncle Steve Roberts, a pioneer and original settler, who has been here 17 years. This house, a two-story gray unpainted shack, and the half dozen or more one-story ones of his sons and in-laws, comprise the settlement. . . . We had brought our lunch with us, but on returning I found King and the family at dinner. They insisted that I join them, which I did in a kitchen which smelled to heaven of cockroach stink. The main items of the meal were wild duck stew, gingerbread and limeade. (1932, 284)

2. While Glen's grandfather made a "good living" cutting buttonwood in the area, this was by no means an easy task. During the same period as Glen's grandfather lived on the Cape cutting buttonwood and shipping it to Key West, Col. Hugh Willoughby recounts meeting a crew of men hauling buttonwood off of East Cape. The captain of the crew, according to Willoughby, asked him to send a small boat to the shore to retrieve his men. Willoughby described this encounter saying,

I found a very dilapidated old craft about fifty feet long that was leaking badly. The captain evidently looked upon us with a great deal of suspicion, having mistaken us for Cuban filibusters. . . . He implored me to let him have a little sugar and coffee, as they were in an almost starving condition, the food having given out two weeks before; his men had been delayed in getting the lumber out, also by the mosquitoes that had infested the place where they were chopping to such an extent that one man nearly lost his life. Their faces and hands certainly bore evidence to the truth of this statement. (1992, 99)

3. John K. Small gives a thorough description of the flora of the prehurricane Cape Sable prairies in his 1929 book entitled *From Eden to Sahara: Florida's Tragedy.* Beginning at Flamingo, Small drove westward, noting,

The great prairies west of Flamingo are bordered by hammocks towards the bay. The hammocks are usually fringed by the Spanish bayonet (*Yucca aloifolis*), often growing in impenetrable thickets without the admixture of other woody plants. The wild cotton also covers acres of prairie land and it is continuously in flower and in fruit the year round. Back of East Cape Sable the hammocks are also fringed with wild armed plants. . . cacti, prickly pears, principally Opuntia Dillenii and dildoe (*Acanthocereus floridanus*). Out that way, too, there are numerous oasis of clumps of cabbage trees (*Sabal*) and of thatch-palm (*Thrinax*). Beyond East Cape we ran to the eastern shore of Whitewater Lake which parallels the shore. . . . We drove parallel with it to its upper end. There the prairies were carpeted with great patches of various shades of green — the gray-green of the sea-oxeye (*Borrichia frutescens*), yellow-green of the sea-purslane (*Sesuvium Portulacastrum*), light-green of the samphire (*Salicornia ambigua*), and red of the sea-blite (*Dondia maritima*). Most of these plants were dwarf and rarely exceeded a foot in height. Between Middle Cape and Northwest Cape we ran through miles of switch-grass (*Spartina*) placed so thick that for hundreds of yards the ground was not visible. . . . (1929, 100–01)

4. Craighead suggests that the construction of the Buttonwood Canal from Flamingo to Coot Bay in 1956 and 1957 may have contributed to the decline of the bay's coot and duck populations. In his *Trees of South Florida*, Craighead both describes and includes photographs of the coots and ducks on Coot Bay prior to the digging of the canal. By introducing salt water

into this pond, the canal caused the destruction of the aquatic flora that supported this water fowl (1971, 6).

5. Duck hawks, or peregrine falcons, hunt by flying through flocks of flying birds and striking them with their clenched talons. Diving speeds of these falcons have been estimated at 175 miles per hour (Wetmore 1965, 23).

6. Lawrence E. Will's *A Dredgeman of Cape Sable* (1967) offers a colorful account of the construction of the Cape Sable Canal.

7. Now the canal at the eastern end of Lake Ingraham is interspersed with a confusing network of mud banks and narrow tidal channels.

8. Stuart C. Hix, in his 1928 book entitled *The Notorious Ashley Gang*, describes the saga of John Ashley's gang, which included John's girlfriend, Laura Upthegrove, the "self styled 'Queen of the Everglades'" (Hix 1928, 22). Hix opens his account saying, "Out of the somber stillness of the Everglades comes this story of John Ashley, bank-robber, highway-man, pirate, hi-jacker and murderer" (1928, 7). John Ashley's eldest sister married Wes Mobley, and their son, Hanford, led the gang's second holdup of the Stuart Bank in 1924. Described by Hix as "frail and effeminate in appearance, Hanford's efforts to emulate his uncle might have occasioned mirth save for the ever present menace of a brace of .38's. Behind the guns his brown squinty eyes snapped fire, the thick lips tightened over clenched teeth, and the youthful countenance gave way to the determined leer of the killer" (1928, 28). Apparently it was Hanford's "effeminate" appearance that allowed him to disguise himself as a woman during the holdup.

9. The Bill Ashley Camp was located about halfway down the Joe River from Oyster Bay. The camp was made on the marsh side (or southwestern side) of the river so that the marsh could be walk-hunted. According to Glen, the Joe River was lined with cabbage palms until at least the 1950s. Now only the dead husks of the stumps remain.

10. Hix notes that Bill Ashley "never took kindly to the operations of the gang and made every effort, it is said, to reform them" (Hix 1928, 58).

11. Hix confirms Glen's interpretation of Bill's and Wes's refuge in the glades. Hix states that after a particularly brutal shoot-out between John Ashley and the sheriff's department (which occurred in 1924 and resulted in John's father's death), "Wesley Mobley was taken into custody and, hearing he was wanted, Bill Ashley surrendered to the police. All were subsequently released as there was no evidence with which to connect them with the shooting" (Hix 1928, 60).

12. The killing of Desoto Tiger in 1911 was the crime for which John Ashley was initially sought.

13. Karl A. Bickel notes that both white settlers and Seminole Indians shared a belief that the Everglades harbored mythic-sized snakes. Bickel, in *The Mangrove Coast*—a book that incidentally contains photographs by Walker Evans—quotes an interview with Uncle Steve Roberts that was initially published in a WPA pamphlet entitled "Seminole Indians in Florida." Roberts, seemingly without jest, relates that the serpent

> "wasn't no legend but a fact. Buster Farrel, an Indian, killed the critter in 1892. . . . Buster was hunting when he come across a trail where the grass was all beat down in a wide path. . . . Pretty soon he spotted the snake. It was more'n a good rifle shot from him but he fired anyhow, and the critter went threshing off in the grass makin' more noise than a hurricane. Buster didn't go to see whether he'd hit it or not remembering the stories about the serpent swallowing Indians whole. Wasn't 'til some days later he seen a flock of buzzards flyin' around the place, and when he went down there he found the snake. The buzzards had tore and scattered the carcass so bad Buster couldn't measure it, but he swore the snake was all of 60 feet long and as big as a barrel. He cut off and kept the jaw bones, which were so big he could open them up and drop them over his body (1942, 233–34).

In an earlier account, Col. Hugh Willoughby recounts a similar tale told to him by his guide, a man named Brewer (1898, 87).

14. Recent studies indicate that since the 1930s, sea levels along Florida's shorelines have been rising at a rate of 20–40 cm/100 years, which is ten times greater than the rate recorded by earlier tide gauge records and the past several thousand years of geologic history (Wanless, Parkinson, and Tedesco 1994, 200). Wanless, Parkinson and Tedesco discuss the impact rising sea levels and catastrophic hurricanes have had on Everglades wetlands, including the accelerated erosion of shore margins and the landward encroachment of marine wetlands (1994).

15. There is no more marsh around Little Madeira Bay today, only mangroves and hammock.

16. Donald Nicholson, writing in the *Florida Naturalist* in 1938, compares the Cape's state after the hurricane to a visit he made in 1927:

> at that time a luxuriant growth of mangroves which fringed the Bay of Florida, and dense growth of tropical and semi-tropical trees and shrubs forming hammocks, with tangles of vicious climbing cactus

... [were] growing profusely. . . . However, now all was changed, and a pitiful transformation greeted those of us who had seen the section prior to the most disastrous tropical storm. . . . The damage to the vegetation was appalling, since fully 98% of all trees had been killed, and the ground was strewn with the wreckage of trees, branches and debris. The havoc wrought by this terrible storm was beyond belief. (1938, 44)

17. Both Tebeau (1963, 9) and Craighead (1964, 10) refer to this stand of black mangroves as the "Black Forest."

18. The sugar cane apparently thrived when it was planted on areas of higher ground on the prairie outside of Flamingo (Simpson 1920, 104).

19. E. J. Watson was a notorious outlaw who lived off the Chatham River in the Ten Thousand Islands. Peter Matthiessen's *Killing Mister Watson* (1990) offers a rich fictionalized account of Mr. Watson's life and death, as well as an insight into the lives of the scattered families living around the outpost town of Chokoloskee.

20. A Category I hurricane reached Florida in October of 1946 (Simpson and Riehl 1981, 371). This may be the storm Glen is describing.

BIBLIOGRAPHY

Allen, E. Ross, and Wilfred T. Neill. 1949. "Increasing Abundance of the Alligator in the Eastern Portion of Its Range." *Herpetologica* 5 (December): 109–12.

Barbour, Thomas. 1947. *That Vanishing Eden: A Naturalist's Florida.* Boston: Little, Brown.

Beard, Daniel B. 1938. *Wildlife Reconnaissance: Everglades National Park Project.* Washington, D.C.

———. 1949. "Wildlife of Everglades National Park." *National Geographic* 95 (January): 83–116.

Beck, W. M. 1939. "The Pinellas County Snake Bounty." *Florida Naturalist* 12 (July): 94.

Behler, John L. 1978. *Feasibility of the Establishment of a Captive-breeding Population of the American Crocodile.* Report T–509. Homestead, Fla.: National Park Service, South Florida Research Center, Everglades National Park.

Bickel, Karl A. 1942. *The Mangrove Coast.* Photographs by Walker Evans. New York: Coward-McCann.

Blatchley, W. S. 1932. *In Days Agone.* Indianapolis: Nature Publishing.

Chapman, Frank M. 1908. *Camps and Cruises of an Ornithologist.* New York: Appleton.

Cory, Charles B. 1896. *Hunting and Fishing in Florida.* Boston: Estes and Lauriat.

Covington, James W. 1993. *The Seminoles of Florida.* Gainesville: University Press of Florida.

Craighead, Frank C., Sr. 1968. "The Role of the Alligator in Shaping Plant Communities and Maintaining Wildlife in the Southern Everglades." *Florida Naturalist* 41 (January–April).

———. 1971. *The Trees of South Florida.* Coral Gables, Fla.: University of Miami Press.

———. 1974. "Land, Mangroves, and Hurricanes." *Fairchild Tropical Garden Bulletin* 19 (October): 1–21.

Cruickshank, Helen G. 1948. *Flight into Sunshine.* Photographs by Allan D. Cruickshank. New York: Macmillan.

Dickinson, W. E. 1953. "In Quest of an Adult Crocodile." *Everglades Natural History* 1 (December): 151–56.

Dimock, A. W. 1926 [1908]. *Florida Enchantments.* Rpt., New York: Frederick A. Stokes.

Federal Writers' Project of the Works Projects Administration for the State of Florida. 1939. *Florida: A Guide to the Southernmost State.* New York: Oxford University Press.

George, Paul S. 1986. "Brokers, Binders, and Builders: Greater Miami's Boom of the Mid–1920s." *Florida Historical Quarterly* 65 (July): 27–51.

Gifford, John D. 1912. *The Everglades and Other Essays Relating to Southern Florida.* 2d ed. Miami: Everglade Land Sales.

Hadley, Alden H. 1941. "Reminiscences of the Florida Everglades." *Florida Naturalist* 14 (January): 21–29.

Hanna, Alfred Jackson, and Kathryn Abbey Hanna. 1948. *Lake Okeechobee: Wellspring of the Everglades.* Indianapolis, Ind.: Bobbs-Merrill.

Harper, Francis, and Delma E. Presley. 1981. *Okefinokee Album.* Athens, Ga.: University of Georgia Press.

Harshberger, John W. 1914. "The Vegetation of South Florida South of 27° 30' North, Exclusive of the Florida Keys." *Transactions of Wagner Free Institute of Science.*

Heilner, Van Campen. 1922. *Adventures in Angling.* Cincinnati: Stewart Kidd.

Hix, Stuart C. 1928. *The Notorious Ashley Gang: A Saga of the King and Queen of the Everglades.* Stuart, Florida: St. Lucie Printing.

Jennings, W. S. 1916. "Royal Palm State Park." *The Tropic Magazine.*

Job, Herbert K. 1905. *Wild Wings.* New York: Houghton Mifflin & Company.

Kersey, Harry A., Jr. 1975. *Pelts, Plumes, and Hides: White Traders among the Seminole Indians, 1870–1930.* Gainesville, Fla.: University Presses of Florida.

———. 1989. *The Florida Seminoles and the New Deal, 1933–1942.* Boca Raton, Fla.: Florida Atlantic University Press.

Lamb, John S., Sr. [Mid–1970s]. Letter written to Tom Martin, Manager of the Loxahatchee National Wildlife Refuge.

Light, Stephen S., and J. Walter Dineen. 1994. "Water Control in the Everglades: A Historical Perspective." In *Everglades: The Ecosystem and Its Restoration,* Steven M. Davis and John C. Ogden, eds. Delray Beach, Fla.: St. Lucie Press.

Matthiessen, Peter. 1990. *Killing Mister Watson.* New York: Random House.

Miami Daily News. 1938. "Law's Hand Stayed in Kidnap Case While Father Who Paid Ransom Pleads for Time." May 31, 1938, sec. 1A, p. 1.

Nicholson, Donald J. 1938. "A Historical Trip to Cape Sable." *The Florida Naturalist* 11 (January): 41–44.

Paige, John C. 1989. *Historical Resource Study for Everglades National Park.* Washington, D.C.: U.S. Department of the Interior, National Park Service.

Parks, Arva Moore. 1986. Introduction to *The Florida Hurricane & Disaster, 1926,* by L. F. Reardon. 1926. Rpt., Coral Cables, Fla.: Arva Moore Parks.

Parks, Pat. 1968. *The Railroad That Died At Sea.* Brattleboro, Vt.: Stephen Greene Press.

Reardon, L. F. 1926. *The Florida Hurricane & Disaster, 1926.* Rpt., Coral Cables, Fla.: Arva Moore Parks, 1986.

Reese, Albert M. 1915. *The Alligator and Its Allies.* New York: G. P. Putnam's Sons.

Reimann, Edward J. 1940. "The Southwest Florida Patrol." *The Florida Naturalist* 13 (July 1940): 73–79.

Robertson, William B., Jr. 1953. "A Survey of the Effects of Fire in Everglades National Park." Washington, D.C.: United States Department of the Interior National Park Service.

Robertson, William B., Jr. 1988. *Everglades: The Park Story.* Homestead, Fla.: Florida National Parks and Monuments Association.

Rowsome, Frank, Jr. 1965. *The Verse by the Side of the Road.* New York: Plume.

Safford, W. E. 1919. "Natural History of Paradise Key and the Near-by Everglades of Florida." *Annual Report of the Board of Regents of the Smithsonian*

Institution: Showing the Operations, Expenditures, and Conditions of the Institution for the Year Ending June 30, 1917. Washington, D.C.: Government Printing Office.

Simpson, Charles Torrey. 1920. *In Lower Florida Wilds.* New York: G. P. Putnam's Sons.

Simpson, Charles Torrey. 1923. *Out of Doors in Florida.* Miami, Fla.: E. B. Douglas.

Simpson, Robert H., and Herbert Riehl. 1981. *The Hurricane and Its Impact.* Baton Rouge: Louisiana State University Press.

Small, John Kunkel. 1929. *From Eden to Sahara: Florida's Tragedy.* Lancaster, Penn.: Science Press Printing.

Small, John K. 1929. "The Everglades." *The Scientific Monthly* 28 (January 1929): 80–87.

Sprunt, Alexander, Jr. October 3, 1935. Unpublished Audubon field notes.

Stimson, Louis A. 1940. "Off the Map." *The Florida Naturalist* 13 (July): 80–82.

Taylor, Jean. n.d. *Villages of South Dade.* St. Petersburg, Fla.: Byron Kennedy.

Tebeau, Charlton W. 1963. *They Lived in the Park.* Coral Gables, Fla.: University of Miami Press.

Tebeau, Charlton W. 1971. *A History of Florida.* Coral Gables, Fla.: University of Miami Press.

Wanless, Harold R., Randall W. Parkinson, and Lenore P. Tedesco. 1990. "Sea Level Control on Stability of Everglades Wetlands." In *Everglades: The Ecosystem and Its Restoration,* Steven M. Davis and John C. Ogden, eds. Delray Beach, Fla.: St. Lucie Press.

Wetmore, Alexander. 1965. "Winged Creatures Through the Ages: The World of Birds." *Water, Prey, and Game Birds of North America.* Washington, D.C.: National Geographic Society.

Will, Lawrence E. 1967. *A Dredgeman of Cape Sable.* St. Petersburg, Fla.: Great Outdoors Publishing.

Willoughby, Hugh. L. 1898. *Across the Everglades.* Rpt., Port Salerno, Fla.: Florida Classics Library, 1992.

INDEX

Black Hammock Camp, 36
Black Woods ("Black Forest"), 156–57
Blatchley, W. S., 123, 124, 182n.1
Bluefield Farms, 117
Blue Goose Farm, 63
Bonita Springs, 111, 113, 182n.15
Bradley, Louis, 29
Bradley Key, 138
Brady, Duncan C., 122, 130, *131*, 145
Brady, Oren, *52*
Break-A-Leg Camp, 36
Brewer Hammock, 8
Broken Bones Camp, 36
Brooker, Ed, 39, 62–63, 106; camp named
  for, 30, 42, 176n.4; hunting with, 26,
  37, 41–46, 51–52, 73; landing named
  for, 29, 55; and pelt and hide trade,
  107, 110
Brooker, Henry, 110
Brooker Lakes, 121
Brooker's Island, 45
Broward, Napoleon Bonaparte, xiv
Brown's Boat landing, 83
Buttonwood Canal, 183n.4
Buttonwood Embankment, 176n.3
Buzzard Camp, 36

Cabbage Trees Camp, 155
Caloosahatchee River, 174n.9
Calusa Indians, 174n.9. *See also* Indians:
  evidence of ancient
Camp Bill Ashley, xii (map), 61, 96, 150,
  153, 184n.9. *See also* Ashley, Bill
Camp Jackson, 174n.7
Camp Jack Trail, 8–9
Camp Nasty, 36, 153
Canal Point (Lake Okeechobee), *101*,
  109, 110
Cape Sable, 27, *30*, 79, 80, 125; ancient
  Indians on, 135, 174n.9; prairies on,
  130, 183n.3; wildlife on, 134–35, 144,
  182n.15
Cape Sable Canal, 144, 184n.6
Cape Sable Prairie, 122–25
Cape Sable Road. *See* Ingraham Highway

Card Sound, 111, 135
Carter, Fishhook, *101*, 107, *109*, 109–10
Cash, James, Sr., 178n.13
Cash, James Bailey, Jr. ("Skeegie"), 67–68,
  178n.13
Casper (hide buyer from St. Augustine),
  107, 108, 113, 139
Cattail Lakes, xii (map), 123, 144, 146–
  49, 160. *See also* Big Cattail Lake;
  Little Cattail Lake
CCC. *See* Civilian Conservation Corps
Central and Southern Florida Project, xv
Chapman, Frank, 29, 178n.14
Chattahoochee, 123
Chicken Farm, 114
Chokoloskee, 130, 186n.19
Civilian Conservation Corps (CCC), 22–
  23
Civil War, 81, 130
Clewiston, 119
Cocoa (town), 81
Coconut Grove, 145
Context Road, 74–75
Coot Bay, xii (map), 138, 149, 183n.4
Coot Bay Hammock, 124, 161, 162
Coot Bay Landing, *150, 154*
Coot Bay Pond, 133, 138, 148
Coot Bay Prairie, 149
Coppinger, Henry, 177n.11
Corps of Engineers, 8, 90
Cory, Charles, 85
Craighead, Frank C., Sr., xx, *52*, 176n.3,
  179nn.14, 20, 183n.4
"Crazy Sam," 136–38
Crooked Lake, 22
Cruickshank, Allan, 126
Cruickshank, Helen, 126, 178n.14
Cuthbert Lake, xii (map), 44, 55, 56, 68–
  74, 89, 100, 176n.3, 179n.14; camp at,
  36; rookery at, xxi, 29, *69,* 69–70
Cuthbert Marsh, 73
Cutler (town), 2, 8, 58

Dade County, 22, 84, 107, 108, 113–14
Davis, Ira, 47, 136, 137